Church Safety And Security

A Practical Guide

Robert M. Cirtin

with

John M. Edie
Dennis K. Lewis
Edward L. Spain
Donna M. Washburn

CSS Publishing Company, Inc., Lima, Ohio

CHURCH SAFETY AND SECURITY

Library of Congress Cataloging-in-Publication Data

Cirtin, Robert M., 1954-
  Church safety and security : a practical guide / Robert M. Cirtin with John M. Edie ...
[et al.].
     p. cm.
  ISBN 0-7880-2341-1 (perfect bound : alk. paper)
  1. Clergy—Professional ethics. 2. Churches—Security measures. 3. Church officers—
Professional ethics. 4. Churches—Safety measures. 5. Crime—Religious aspects—
Christianity. I. Title.
  BV4011.5.C57 2005
  254—dc22
                                                                    2005001767

For more information about CSS Publishing Company resources, visit our website at
www.csspub.com or e-mail us at custserv@csspub.com or call (800) 241-4056.

Cover design by Chris Patton
ISBN 0-7880-2341-1   PRINTED IN U.S.A.

This book is dedicated to the victims of misconduct perpetrated by church leaders and of church violence, as well as the many church leaders and workers whose commitment to God compels them to do what is right.

Disclaimer

The recommendations contained in this book are not intended to be legal advice. The purpose of this book is provide general recommendations regarding safety and security issues as they relate to churches, and to stimulate discussion among church leaders and within congregations. Any questions of a legal nature should be directed to appropriate legal counsel. The author and publisher are not responsible for any actions taken as a result of the contents of this book.

Although male pronouns are used throughout this book, for consistency, these pronouns are meant to apply to all people and not be gender-specific.

Table Of Contents

Acknowledgments

I wish to express my thanks and appreciation to the following:

My wife, Brenda, and daughters, Angela and Jennifer, for their unconditional love and support throughout our wonderful journey together.

My mother and father, Arnold and Betty Cirtin, for instilling in me the spiritual foundation and work ethic I needed to get where I am today.

Contributing authors, John Edie, Dennis Lewis, Eddie Spain, and Donna Washburn for their commitment to God and for sharing their expertise to make the church a safer place in which to worship God.

Jacob Nunnally who was able to take our words and make them sound even better.

And finally, I wish to thank Almighty God for his continual faithfulness to me and my family, and for providing a means to utilize my love for law enforcement, Christian ministry, and teaching, for him.

Introduction

It is regrettable that a book of this nature is necessary, but in today's society it is. Even though we think of church as a safe place to give and receive ministry, there have been several recent examples to show that it is safe no longer. I understand that many church leaders might think, "It could never happen in our church, and moreover we should continue to trust God to provide for our safety." The purpose of this book is not to overreact to recent problems, but to assist churches in becoming prepared. It is not prudent to take safety and security measures to the extreme, but we must also be good stewards of what God has entrusted to us in the way of people and buildings.

We have many instances of members of the pastoral staff and other church leaders displaying unethical, illegal, and sinful conduct. This book contains many convincing examples of this reality that will illustrate the need for this book.

Church leaders must find a balance between providing for the safety and security of those who enter the church doors, providing a peaceful and safe place that is a shelter from the outside world, and a place that is a spiritual sanctuary to those in need. Too often, church leaders and congregations have been reactive instead of proactive; due to changes in our society, this is no longer sufficient.

Many problems that occur in the church have harmful affects on their congregations and even on entire denominations. Churches and denominations are liable for what occurs in the church and are targets of lawsuits now more than ever. While it may be impossible to totally prevent misconduct at a given church, there are steps that church leaders and congregations can take to reduce the risk and to appropriately deal with these issues.

Both pastors and congregations can be negatively impacted by harm done to victims of misconduct by those in church. Not only the physical and emotional impact on the victim of misconduct, but the spiritual impact on the victims of misconduct can all

9

have an adverse impact on the entire congregation and denomination. The adverse news coverage that may ensue, the financial costs of litigation and possible financial judgment against the church, and the negative impact it could have on the congregation and the community is too great to simply trust that "it won't happen to us."

My hope is that this book will promote discussion among church leaders and congregations that will ultimately result in a safer place in which people can come to worship God. God is still in control and his protection is still available to us. We should continue to trust in him, but at the same time, we must also utilize the common sense and resources that God has given us.

As a former police officer, an investigator, and one who has participated in full-time church ministry, I understand the problems facing the church today regarding safety and security. It is my prayer that this book will help provide a safe environment to worship God.

Robert M. Cirtin

Chapter 1

Protect Your Congregation By Using Background Screening

Robert M. Cirtin, B.A., M.A.

Paul told the Ephesians, "Have nothing to do with the fruitless deeds of darkness, but rather expose them." Paul acknowledged that it is shameful to talk about what the disobedient do in secret, adding, "Everything exposed by the light becomes visible, for it is the light that makes everything visible."

During the past twenty years misconduct by those participating in church ministry has dramatically increased. As a result, civil lawsuits and negative media attention have also increased. These incidents are devastating to the persons involved, their families, the church, the denomination, and the community. When misconduct occurs, however, church and denominational leaders often fail to deal adequately with the perpetrators. If the situation is dealt with, perpetrators are sometimes quietly removed from their positions of leadership and allowed to serve other congregations.

Examples

Consider these real-life examples. William Michael Altman, senior pastor of Grace Christian Ministries, a nondenominational church, became involved in a sexual relationship with a parishioner whom he was counseling for issues pertaining to being a victim of molestation as a child, as well as depression and eating disorders. Reverend Altman visited the parishioner in the hospital after a third suicide attempt. Reverend Altman confessed to church leaders and stated that the relationship was a consensual affair.

If a simple background investigation had been conducted on Michael Altman prior to his appointment as pastor, it would have revealed that he had been in prison for falsifying a $50,000 loan application. Also, it would have revealed that he was asked to resign by two former congregations.

While working as an associate pastor of a church in Groton, Massachusetts, in 1991, Michael Cranford was convicted of indecent assault and battery on a boy. Due to his conviction, he was barred from working for, or volunteering with, organizations that work with children under the age of eighteen. He subsequently moved to New Hampshire where in January of 2002 he was charged with sexually assaulting a fourteen-year-old boy in Candia, New Hampshire, sometime between September 1996 and June 1997.

After learning of the case in Candia, police in Raymond, New Hampshire, began an investigation into allegations that Cranford sexually assaulted another boy of approximately fourteen years of age between January 1995 and December 1996. He was eventually indicted. When these charges were filed, he was serving as an associate pastor of a church in Raymond. As can be expected, Cranford failed to tell church officials that he was a convicted sex offender in Massachusetts. The church terminated his employment upon learning of the charges.

Afterward, Michael Cranford applied to work with children in a fire department's "Explorer" post without disclosing his conviction for sexual assault. He was later charged with prohibitions of childcare service because he continued to work with children in his position as youth pastor and with the Candia Fire Department's Explorer program for high schoolers.

It is illustrative that the church in Raymond conducted a criminal history check in New Hampshire, which showed that Cranford had no criminal convictions in that state. Of course, this did not reveal the conviction in Massachusetts.

A survey conducted by *Church Law and Tax Report* found that church volunteers commit fifty percent of all incidents of sexual abuse in churches, paid staff commit thirty percent of such incidents, and other children commit twenty percent.

Now, more than ever before, it is important for churches to make a reasonable investigation into the fitness of those they allow to participate in church ministry. This chapter pertains to all positions in the church, whether financially compensated or not.

12

Included are the senior pastor, pastoral staff, youth leaders, clerical and other support staff, custodians, and the many volunteers such as Sunday school teachers and nursery workers.

This is a very sensitive subject because it is unpleasant for churches to think about screening potential staff. We want to trust the people we place in leadership positions and trust that their backgrounds reflect the integrity and holiness expected of those desiring to do God's work. The problem is that some people are not honest, even those who profess a relationship with God. Therefore, it is the responsibility of church leaders to discover if a person's background is not what it is purported to be.

As the previous examples illustrate, we are aware of many situations in which those who provide services at a church, both compensated and volunteer, have committed acts that are inappropriate, sinful, and sometimes even criminal. In fact, court cases have held that an employer could be liable for acts committed by an employee even when the behavior is beyond the scope of the person's duties.

To complicate matters even more, churches must take a close look at individuals who have committed crimes or other inappropriate behavior prior to conversion. Of course, forgiveness has been granted, but the church has no obligation to place them in leadership positions that will jeopardize the safety of others. However, depending on the pre-conversion behavior, these people may be used in positions unrelated to the acts they committed. For example, for one convicted of theft, such an individual might be used in a ministry of the church that does not allow access to money or valuable property.

Negligent Employment Decisions

Negligent hiring and negligent retention are concepts with which church leaders must become familiar. Negligent hiring is more than just *respondeat superior*. This concept states that employers are responsible for their employees while they are working at the direction of the business, which in this case would be the church. The term "negligent hiring," according to Applicant Insight, Ltd., is different from *respondeat superior* in that it indicates that an employer owes a duty to coworkers, customers, and the public at large. The employer can be sued for harmful acts committed by an employee if the company failed to adequately research that employee's background. Negligent hiring theory assumes that if the employer had investigated an employee's past, that person's history of antisocial or criminal behavior would have been discovered. Therefore, the employer should not have placed such an employee in a position to harm others.

This means that if an employer hires an applicant without confirming the information the applicant provided, and it is later discovered that the individual has a background indicating a propensity for misconduct, the employer could be liable if the employee commits a crime or displays other inappropriate conduct while on the job.

Negligent hiring enables plaintiffs to recover damages from a church in many situations in which they ordinarily could not. It is also one of the biggest problems facing employers today and must be addressed by churches and church organizations.

Negligent retention occurs when a church retains employees or volunteers with knowledge of their unfitness, and they later cause harm or injury to others. Liability is created when the church retains unethical, dangerous, or otherwise unsatisfactory employees or volunteers.

Many church leaders make the mistake of ignoring problems of behavior exhibited by paid staff and volunteers in the hope they will disappear. Some even become unwitting accomplices by looking the other way, thereby condoning such behavior. This is indeed both ridiculous and irrational. Church leaders should make employment decisions based on investigation and logic rather than by good feelings and wishful thinking. For example, if church leaders become aware that one of the bus drivers has an unsatisfactory driving record and fails to relieve that bus driver of his or her duties, the church could be liable for negligent retention.

The Issue Of Liability

In our litigious society, businesses, as well as churches, have a duty to protect the congregation and staff from those who might pose a risk of harm. In addition, the church must also be concerned about the possible consequences of failing to conduct adequate background investigations of individuals they allow to participate in church ministry, again, both salaried and volunteer.

In fact, churches are legally responsible for both paid and volunteer workers and can be liable if they fail to uncover a person's incompetence or unfitness for a particular position. This entails taking proactive steps to protect the public and prevent a successful lawsuit. Whether we like to think about the church in this way or not, the church is, after all, a business, and therefore must be operated utilizing certain business principles.

We have become aware that the number of lawsuits that have been filed against churches, clergy, and denominations as a result of sexual abuse is increasing. This is particularly a concern for churches because there is evidence that suggests that pedophiles volunteer to work in church ministries involving children in order to have easy access to children.

The purpose of this chapter is not to give legal advice, but to make churches aware of the legal liability imposed by negligent hiring and negligent retention. I recommend that churches consult legal counsel familiar with the relevant statutes in the states where they are situated.

Church denominational leaders and congregations can actively lessen the possibility of hiring individuals who may have the propensity for inappropriate behavior. By conducting background-screening procedures on paid and volunteer staff, the church and the denomination can decrease the risk and liability in hiring and promotion decisions. Churches can achieve a level of comfort that the people they hire or appoint are the people they say they are and are expected to be.

With respect to volunteers, many churches will select anyone who expresses an interest in working in a volunteer capacity without conducting any type of screening procedure. After all, it is sometimes difficult to attract volunteer workers, so the church does not want to insult people or make it troublesome for them to become involved in the ministries of the church. This attitude can only lead to trouble.

It helps church leaders if they think of screening procedures in terms of reducing legal risk. When a church hires workers without any screening or evaluation of candidates, this involves the highest degree of risk. The converse is also true: when a church utilizes a screening process for selecting church workers, risk is reduced.

Any screening procedure is designed to provide a safe and secure environment for the congregation. Establishing a screening procedure is a small price to pay for protecting the church from employees and volunteers who exhibit inappropriate or illegal behavior.

Background Investigation And
Pre-employment Screening

These terms, "background investigation" and "pre-employment screening," are used for pre-employment, employment, and general screening which can assess an individual's reputation and past job performance. It is vital for a church to uncover any gaps in employment or other undisclosed information in the individual's past. Information gathered for a background investigation is compiled by utilizing computer databases, but personal interviews are sometimes required, depending on the extent of the inquiry.

It is very important to obtain background information from the sources of the information. There are many pre-employment screening or investigative companies that provide this information. However, some companies obtain the information from a vendor whose information may be outdated or inaccurate. Therefore, it is necessary to ensure that the information received is from the source of that information. For example, if a criminal record search is needed in the state in which the individual resides, the search should come directly from the state. In my state, Missouri,

16

my company obtains criminal history checks directly from the Missouri State Highway Patrol, which serves as the repository for state level criminal convictions.

Assume that a church is in the process of recruiting a youth pastor. The final successful applicant is about to be offered the position. If it becomes known that the candidate was previously convicted of sexually molesting a teenager, would this influence the decision to hire this person as the youth pastor? Of course it would. Why do churches employ paid staff and volunteers with no consideration of their backgrounds other than the information provided by the candidates? Reasonable background screening can avoid many potential problems.

It is important to know what you are getting. As previously stated, if a state criminal history search is conducted on an individual, only state convictions in that particular state will be known. It is important to know this because a person may have committed a federal crime, a misdemeanor in a municipal jurisdiction, or a crime in another state. Many drug related offenses are prosecuted in federal court. If this is the case, by only conducting a state criminal check you will have no knowledge of the other convictions in federal court, the various municipal courts, or other states. There is no nationwide criminal history check available to the public that will provide information on all criminal convictions in every jurisdiction.

For this reason, I recommend a Social Security verification or address verification search. These searches can provide previous locations in which the person has lived. This can be significant because the applicant may be concealing a criminal conviction in another state by not revealing that he lived in that state.

Performing various screening checks is beneficial for several reasons. They will deter high-risk individuals from applying for positions in the church, and they may identify applicants with a history of inappropriate conduct. This will enable church leaders to reject them, or perhaps appoint them and provide appropriate safeguards. Also, having a screening procedure in place demonstrates to everyone in the church and denomination a concern for the safety and security of the congregation.

Please be aware that no background screening is foolproof. For example, I once conducted a criminal search in the State of Missouri for a person I was investigating. The result of my inquiry indicated that the subject had no criminal convictions. During the course of my investigation I discovered that at the time I conducted the inquiry the person was incarcerated in a Missouri prison. How did this slip through the system? Not all of the counties and municipalities report criminal convictions to the state agency responsible for collecting the information; in this case, the Missouri State Highway Patrol. The respective state agency responsible for maintaining criminal records can only provide information that is reported to them.

Courts have not provided a list of the types of background checks that should be completed. The word "reasonableness" has been used by our nation's courts when describing information that an employer would be expected to investigate.

Church leaders can select from an extensive menu of reasonably available background screening searches that can be customized to suit specific needs. The following pages provide a list and description of the most beneficial and widely used components of background investigations from which to choose.

State and county criminal history

You can obtain a report detailing felony and misdemeanor convictions directly from the applicable state. Information is available from all fifty states. In many states the information is offered on a statewide search basis, while in others a county search must be conducted in order to identify the outstanding criminal record. A criminal check should be performed in every jurisdiction the person has lived as an adult. Please note that obtaining information about arrest records is not permissible. An arrest alone does not prove that the person committed a crime. Research into an applicant's criminal history must include a reasonable number of jurisdictions in which the applicant has resided.

Federal court criminal history

Because more cases such as drug charges, embezzlement, and mail and wire fraud are being tried within the federal court system, it has become important to conduct a complete federal criminal conviction search. This search will provide information about criminal activity in the Federal District Courts in the United States. The federal court search is separate from statewide, countywide, or municipal searches.

Municipal court criminal history

An individual may not have been convicted of a state criminal offense but possibly was convicted in a city court. Many traffic offenses, peace disturbances, trespassing charges, and a host of other misdemeanor crimes are prosecuted in municipal courts. In order to obtain this information, a search from a relevant municipal court is required.

Social Security number verification

A growing problem in the United States is identity theft. Now more than ever it is important to positively identify the person who is applying for a paid or volunteer position in your church. A Social Security number verification search can verify the authenticity of the individual's Social Security number, confirm the name, state of issue, date of issue, and will usually provide the individual's current and some previous addresses. It can also indicate if the Social Security number in question appears on the files of the deceased or misused lists of the Social Security Administration.

This search will reveal any aliases used by the person and a complete list of addresses associated with the person's name.

Social Security number verification can be significant because applicants might not disclose that they lived in a state or city where they committed a crime. By failing to disclose where they previously lived and committed a crime, you would have no way of knowing that conducting a criminal check in that city or state is warranted. Conducting Social Security verification might solve this problem.

Sex offender records search

This search will reveal if the person is listed in a state's sex offender's database. The databases are developed according to the statutes in each state. Most databases consist of the names and related data of sex offenders and sexually violent predators who are not in prison. Please know that not all states participate in this program.

Credit history report

Sometimes the truth is unpleasant; still, it must be sought. What if a church hires a pastor, or employs an administrator, a book-keeper, or others who have financial responsibility yet cannot successfully administer their own personal finances? A credit check will provide guidance in this regard and much more.

According to Applicant Insight, Ltd., some people will argue that information, which is reasonably available to an employer, may be an invasion of a person's privacy. Some claim that a person's credit report, as such, is an invasion of privacy. After all, why would any employer, including a church, need to delve into prospective employees' financial history, especially if their jobs do not require them to handle money or the church's financial records? Even though this logic seems to be well founded, it has no merit in the context of conducting diligent background investigations. It is agreed that if the credit report is being reviewed for the limited purpose of evaluating a person's credit worthiness, there should be some relationship to the person's job duties. However, in light of the fact that the church needs to discover as much information as it can about a potential employee by availing itself of all reasonable sources of information, a credit history check is relevant and can provide insight into a person's true identity and character.

The information obtained through a credit bureau is full of information that goes beyond whether or not a person handles his own finances appropriately. A credit report verifies the person's identity by use of the Social Security number, provides information on previous addresses that were undisclosed where criminal court records may be found, indicates if the person is utilizing a Social Security number that was not issued to him or was issued to someone who is deceased, indicates if he has liens or civil court judgments against him, lists other names used by the person that were not disclosed under which criminal or civil court activity may exist, and provides information on indebtedness, child support, bankruptcy, and wage garnishments. A credit report can reveal much about an individual such as trustworthiness, stability, and responsibility.

Credit history information is reasonably available and can serve as yet another tool to assist the church in determining the character and integrity of the potential church leader.

According to *CCH Business Owner's Toolkit*, there are several things to remember when obtaining a credit history report. Federal law governs the use and disclosure of credit information. If you are going to obtain a credit report, you must obey the applicable federal laws. There are a number of states with laws that require employers to provide notice or copies of credit reports whenever they are used for employment related decisions. Finally, there are anti-discrimination laws that require you to show a business reason for the credit check if screening has a disproportionate impact on minorities.

Motor vehicle records

A motor vehicle records report may not apply to all persons in consideration for a position in your church, but it is necessary for anyone who drives a vehicle while conducting church business. However, even if the person's duties do not include driving vehicles, a driving record report may reveal a pattern of drug and alcohol abuse.

A review of an individual's driving record will show all traffic convictions within the past three to five years and verify the status, classification, and restrictions of the driver's license. This report can reveal a propensity for recklessness and being under the influence of drugs or alcohol. A motor vehicle records check will also verify the person's identity and undisclosed addresses in states where the applicant may have been convicted of a crime.

Civil court history

A criminal court conviction can be characterized as a "public wrong," a wrongful act performed against society. A civil court judgment is characterized as a "private wrong," a wrongful act against an individual. When conducting a civil court records check, you will obtain information on civil court judgments, liens, and lawsuits. This search will determine if an individual was involved in civil proceedings either as plaintiff or defendant.

The church may not want to give a position of responsibility to an individual who has been successfully sued in civil court for behavior that may be relevant to the position under consideration.

Previous employment verification

This background check is used primarily for paid staff, including pastoral and support staff. It has been found that the majority of resumes contain errors, omissions, and false statements. The previous employment verification check can be used to screen entry-level through upper-level positions in the church or denomination.

Former employers are a good source of information regarding the applicant's work history. Information obtained includes, but is not limited to, dates of employment, character, work habits, salary, job title, performance and productivity, attitude, skills, attendance, eligibility for rehire, and reasons for ending employment. It is also a good idea to contact references that are developed through the initial phases of the background investigation. Many churches and businesses do not do any checking and often regret this decision.

Sometimes previous employers will only provide dates of employment and job titles because they are fearful that the candidate might sue them. If this occurs, some states consider this "qualifiedly privileged" and the employer who shares it is protected unless the information is given with known falsity, in bad faith, or with a reckless disregard for the truth (*CCH Business Owner's Toolkit*).

Questions must focus on the applicant's integrity, honesty, criminal history, and propensity for violence, substance abuse, and other behavioral problems.

The preferred method of obtaining previous employer information is by simply using the telephone. This is a quick method, and, additionally, you get "better" information by talking directly with the person. There are, however, some advantages to writing to employers. You can send the employer the written release you obtained from the applicant, and a written response provides documentation that proves what you did.

Whenever the background investigation process begins, it must be remembered that there may be questions you cannot legally ask previous employers. You can avoid doing so by familiarizing yourself with the laws governing such practices in your state.

The persons to interview should include the applicant's former supervisors or other responsible people who will be truthful and whose relationship with the applicant placed them in a position to provide an objective evaluation.

Education and training verification

Education credentials are frequently misrepresented on resumes and job applications. The reason is that many employers, including churches, simply do not verify an applicant's educational achievements. Obviously, it is important for the applicant to have the qualifications, including education that is required for the position. Common misrepresentations include applicants claiming to have college degrees they don't have, or they claim to have degrees from institutions they attended but did not complete the degree. Another common misrepresentation is that the applicant claims to have a degree in one area but actually has a degree in a different one.

This background check will confirm the academic background claimed by the applicant. The report can verify graduation from high school, vocational training center, colleges, and universities. Many employers, including churches, may only want to verify the highest level of academic achievement. This may include dates attended, major and minor, year of graduation, grade point average, degree, diploma, or certificate received, and any special achievements.

23

It may also be necessary to obtain an official copy of the individual's transcript and to verify the accreditation of the institution. It is important to ensure that the degree was not obtained from a college or university that was not appropriately accredited or from a "diploma mill."

Professional licensure verification

Assume that a church seeks to hire a professional counselor or psychologist to provide counseling services to the congregation. It is vital to verify the person's licensure. Any license issued by a governmental agency can be verified for dates of issue, expiration, and any disciplinary action that may have been exacted against the license holder.

Worker's compensation report

Upon seeing the name of this type of background verification, you may be thinking, "Why would a worker's compensation report be necessary for hiring people for positions in a church?" Here's why: This background check identifies applicants who have filed worker's compensation claims and their dispositions against previous employers in the state searched. Thus, a worker's compensation search can detect a propensity for fraudulent claim activity by identifying persons who may intentionally seek opportunities to file worker's compensation claims. It is important to note that under the Americans With Disabilities Act, employers must make a conditional offer of employment prior to receiving worker's compensation records due to specific privacy acts. In addition, these records must be kept confidential.

Public records search

A search of public records is a general search that can provide information that the previous "specific" searches may not provide. This search may include Social Security number, date of birth, aliases used, identity verification, possible addresses linked to the person under consideration for employment, physical description, corporate affiliations, vehicles owned, telephone listings, military records, deed transfers, asset searches, other searches associated with the person's address, and many more.

Personal reference check

Most of the time checking an applicant's personal references is of little value. Personal references are typically friends and family members of the applicant, and they usually will not convey any negative information, if it exists, because they are friends and family. As suggested by *CCH Business Owner's Toolkit*, if you do check personal references, keep in mind that there may be a problem if the applicant cannot provide any local references and he/she has lived in that area for a considerable period of time. Ask only job related questions, thus avoiding irrelevant questions that could lead to a claim of discrimination or support a claim of invasion of privacy.

It is also suggested that you call or speak to the personal reference in person as opposed to writing a letter requesting information. By talking to the person you will get more information by engaging in a conversation.

Utilization of a personal reference check may not be applicable to hiring or appointing church leadership and staff, but it can be very beneficial when conducting an investigation of an incident or event that has occurred in a church or the denomination. A personal reference check may also provide leads that can be pursued in order to obtain additional information.

Conclusion

It is recommended that the church compile a written policy manual, establishing guidelines for hiring paid staff and appointing volunteer staff as well as providing job descriptions for each position. This will ensure that a selection and screening process will be followed that can be applied to everyone. This will maintain consistency in the hiring process.

It is a good idea to have applicants for paid and volunteer positions complete a written application. This should include new and current staff. By screening current staff and volunteers, the church can achieve an added level of comfort and show consistency in its hiring procedures. The application should request information about employment history and references, but it is also important to ask questions about an applicant's criminal record. The application should include a statement for the applicant to sign that certifies that the information provided in the application is complete and accurate, and that falsifying information may lead to rejection of the application or termination. In addition, the application should include a statement that gives consent to conduct a background investigation.

The application process and background investigation could have a deterrent affect. If applicants become upset by having to complete an application or having their background screened, they may have a history that would eliminate them from working in the church. Knowledge of the process may also prevent unscrupulous individuals from seeking a leadership position in the church.

Another good idea is to develop a policy that restricts eligibility for any volunteer position within the church to members in good standing for a period of six to twelve months. This allows church leadership to evaluate individuals prior to their participation in the work of the church.

In the event of a lawsuit, or merely to protect the church in case the church worker later proves unsatisfactory, you must document each step of your background check. This will demonstrate that the church acted reasonably in hiring or appointing the person based on the information you had available at that time.

It is recommended that this information be maintained in a file along with the person's application that can be retrieved later if necessary. It is important that the information collected on the applicant and the documents obtained are maintained in complete confidentiality. The church or denomination should also keep files of individuals who were not hired as paid staff or appointed as volunteers in the event there are any questions at a later date.

Many of these background checks can be done by the church, but it is better to use an objective, unbiased third party that is aware of the laws regulating background investigations and how to conduct them. It also removes the church and its leadership from having personal involvement in the process.

Churches may want to consider hiring professionals who specialize in conducting background investigations. This allows the church to refute later claims that it failed to use reasonable efforts to check into the person's background. There are many reputable public record companies as well as investigative firms, including my company, Robert Cirtin Investigations, L.L.C., who can provide background information at nominal fees. You may contact us at www.cirtininvestigations.com or our safety website at www.safeatchurch.com.

Chapter 2

Threats Of Violence And The Church: A Modern Perspective

Robert M. Cirtin, B.A., M.A.

It is a sad reality of our society that we, as the body of Christ, must consider the possibility that someone may enter a church for the purpose of committing acts of violence against God's people. The church is thought of as a place of safety, a sanctuary for millions of people needing spiritual shelter from the problems of the world, and a place for the body of Christ to worship and to meet the needs of our communities. In order for the church to fulfill the Great Commission, churches must be welcoming to those who desire a closer relationship with God. Of all the places where people should be safe, certainly, it is the church. In days past, violence against others was something that occurred at home, work, or school. Today, because of too many recent examples, we are forced to consider the formerly inconceivable thought of violence in church.

The purpose of this chapter is to assist church leaders and congregations to prepare for the occasion of someone entering their church for the purpose of committing a disturbance or an act of violence. Since the church is "open to the public," the stark reality is that it is impossible to totally prevent violent acts or other disturbances from occurring. However, there are measures churches can implement that can minimize the risk of an intruder causing harm and deal with such an incident when it occurs.

As you read this chapter, and in fact this entire book, you may have a tendency to think "This could not happen in our church. God will take care of us." But when we take a look at scripture, Proverbs 22:3 tells us, "A prudent man sees danger and takes refuge, but the simple keep going and suffer for it." This is good counsel for us today. It is important that churches become proactive instead of reactive when considering these issues and it is hoped that this chapter is conducive in beginning the process.

An illustration may make this point clear. On September 15, 1999, a man entered Wedgewood Baptist Church in Fort Worth, Texas, located in a quiet middle-class neighborhood, and was armed with a 9mm handgun. He stormed into the church, cursing God and shouting anti-religious rhetoric. He killed seven people and injured seven more before shooting himself in the head. The intruder shot at least 45 rounds from his handgun and possessed 100 more rounds of ammunition and two other guns. Oddly enough, the man had six full magazines left when he shot himself in the head. After the incident, when his home was searched, bomb-making equipment including black gunpowder and hundreds of pipe fittings were found. This strange, real-life story illustrates the fact that the church is vulnerable to such an attack; as we will soon see, preparation is the best way to prevent an incident such as this.

Preparing To Prevent

In nearly any imaginable situation in life, one will find that at least some amount of preparation and knowledge working together with what one might call aforethought, would be able to possibly prevent and resolve a certain situation. For example, if someone is aware of the facts (knowledge) of how a car engine works, he will be able to prevent it from running out of oil (aforethought), for he would know how much oil the car uses, where the oil pan and oil filter are both located, and other details. If this same person is driving in his car and the oil pressure suddenly drops to zero and the car begins to break down, the knowledgeable and prepared individual will be able to respond quickly, rationally, and effectively to resolve the problem. He, for instance, would have extra quarts of oil, an extra oil filter, and other necessities on hand, since this individual is aware of the possibility that he might need them at any random time.

This is an illustration of how knowledge of the facts can work in conjunction with aforethought, ending in a fruitful resolution to a given situation. As one may easily see, the protection of churches works in quite a similar manner. If the individual in the example did not have knowledge or aforethought, he/she would be in a heap of unnecessary trouble. Shunning knowledge and aforethought in the realm of church security will bring this same result for church leaders.

If the church has followed the recommendations of chapter 6 and has established a church security team program, this is a good place to begin preparing for and preventing criminal activity. A highly visible security team can prove to be a significant deterrent. As addressed in chapter 6, the security team is not a legally empowered police force charged with the responsibility of watching every move made by every individual who enters the church, but are members of the congregation who have some affinity for security procedures who provide for the safety and security of the congregation. Please see chapter 6 for duties and responsibilities of a church security team.

In addition to the security team members, ushers and greeters can also be trained on how to detect angry or otherwise agitated people and what things for which to be on the alert. These front-line staff members can be very valuable by observing people's behavior and demeanor to possibly detect a person who may have the propensity for violence or who may cause a disturbance.

Proper preplanning and training are essential to the preparation for, and the hopeful prevention of, dangerous incidents. According to Ralph Witherspoon, CPP, of Witherspoon Security Consulting, it is vital that every paid and volunteer staff member is trained and informed of the potential threats to the congregation, as well as their responsibilities to address the threats. The leadership of the church should reinforce established security policies and procedures with all staff members, paid and volunteer. Mr. Witherspoon makes the following excellent recommendations:

- All staff members should be educated on the church's security plan and their specific roles and duties. Every staff member should know how and when to contact local law enforcement.

- One staff member should be appointed as the church security manager (as addressed in ch. 6). Where possible, the security manager should receive training in crime prevention and function as the "in-house expert" but also as the point of contact for all security related information.
- Staff members or church security officers should be assigned to regularly check specific areas.
- Mechanical aspects of the church facility such as lighting and locks should be regularly inspected to ensure that they are operational.
- Evacuation procedures should be established and all staff regularly trained in implementing them. Drills designed to practice evacuation should be held at least twice per year.
- All staff members, including ushers and security officers, should be watchful for strangers loitering around the premises, including those sitting in cars. When observed, they should write down descriptions and if possible, license numbers, and immediately report them to the staff member who serves as the security manager. If that person is not immediately available, local police should be contacted in order to check out the individual.
- A screening procedure for visitors and delivery persons should be implemented during office hours during the week. The purpose is to prevent unscreened strangers from entering the building unnoticed. All staff members should have responsibilities and duties in this critical function.

According to Witherspoon, the "overall thrust of these suggested policies and procedures are to train facility staff and the lay community to recognize unusual activity or persons, to report them in a timely manner, and to be prepared to react appropriately in a planned manner in the event an emergency does occur."

The concepts we have been discussing have been general in nature; the remainder of this chapter will address them specifically.

What to do when a menacing or dangerous intruder who is armed with a weapon enters the church during times of worship

The New St. John Fellowship Baptist Church in the small town of Gonzales, Louisiana, was the sight of a fatal shooting. After noticing him, two men hurried into the church to warn the congregation that a man was coming toward the church with a gun. Nevertheless, the gunman burst into the church and fired a 9mm handgun at his estranged wife and their two-year-old son. Both were instantly killed alongside another congregation member seated next to them. He then randomly shot at the sixty to seventy members who were gathered for a Wednesday night prayer meeting. Four other church members were wounded in this shooting rampage. Just minutes after the shooting occurred, the police cornered the perpetrator in a shed and negotiated with him for over an hour, at which point a sharpshooter shot his gun out of his hand.

Anyone who discovers an intruder or threatening individual should immediately notify the staff member in charge of security. This person will notify the police. The purpose of this is to allow the staff member in charge of security to make the determination if the situation warrants contacting the police and to establish a clear-cut chain of command to adequately manage the incident. If it is obvious that the intruder has some type of weapon in his possession, then whoever observes this should contact the police immediately (so as to have the police respond as quickly as possible) and then notify the staff member in charge of church security.

In the event the intruder is armed with a weapon or claims to have a weapon that is not in view, in most cases it is best to obey all of his demands and instructions. It is important for all involved to remain calm because panic will only exacerbate the situation.

If the intruder has immediate control of people, each individual will have to decide what action to take, if any. An analysis of previous incidents indicates that if the intruder orders individuals to a specific area of confinement, or an abduction occurs, this may significantly increase the possible danger to those involved. In these types of cases, each person must make their own decision with regard to continuing to obey the demands of the intruder or to resist and attempt to escape. If the intruder has already begun using

33

the weapon or is in the process of using the weapon, an attempt to escape and resist may be the only viable options.

Having said this, the following is a list of actions that can be taken in the event of an armed intruder who has entered the church building.

- Do not attempt to confront or subdue an intruder armed with any type of weapon.
- If the intruder is actively shooting a gun, all persons in the immediate area should lie on the floor and if possible, do so in a location of cover and concealment such as under a pew or behind a table.
- If possible to do so safely, anyone who may be near an exit should immediately leave the building or that area of the building.
- If safety permits, church staff members charged with the responsibilities of security (pastoral staff, security officers, and ushers), should instruct people to flee the area to a locality of safety or go to lockable classrooms and offices located away from the perpetrator. Lock the doors to classrooms and offices but be careful not to prevent others from securing protection from the intruder.
- Once inside a secure room or building, using materials that may be available, cover any glass windows of classrooms or offices to prevent the intruder from seeing in.
- If applicable, close shades or curtains on exterior windows.
- Turn off all lights.
- Sit or lie on the floor away from windows and remain quiet.
- Do not leave a secured classroom, office, or building without approval from the police or the staff member in charge of security.
- No one should be allowed to leave a secured classroom, office, or building until instructed to do so by the police or staff member in charge of security for the church.
- Anyone who knows the whereabouts or route of the intruder should direct people to other routes or means of escape.

- If possible to do safely, lock exterior doors to unaffected buildings to prevent entry by the intruder.
- Keep everyone away from the building where the intruder is located.
- Anyone remaining outside should be kept away from the area of the endangered building by security and taken to an unaffected building.
- Members of the congregation and staff in other buildings on the church campus, or in other parts of the building who are unaffected by the crisis should be instructed to remain inside and sit quietly in locked classrooms or offices. If classrooms and offices are unable to be locked, staff members in charge of security should begin evacuating those areas as long as it is safe to do so without being detected by the perpetrator.

What to do when a menacing or dangerous intruder who is *not* armed with a weapon enters the church during times of worship

In this type of situation, one would normally include a person who is in an intoxicated or drugged condition, suffers from an obvious mental disease or defect, or is otherwise disturbed or agitated by something or someone that is not readily apparent. It is important to remember that because the church is a sanctuary for troubled people, a haven of safety in a lost world, and a place of worship to the spiritually needy, there may be some who enter the church who may appear to have subversive intentions but in reality have no such intentions. The following recommendations call for us to proceed with caution.

- If at any time the person makes comments or displays behavior that indicates that he may be a danger to themselves or someone else, the police should be notified immediately.
- If the person is in an obvious intoxicated or drugged condition, notify the police immediately. The behavior of such a person can be volatile and unpredictable, and therefore, potentially dangerous.

35

- If it is safe to do so, either the staff member who is responsible for security or a member of the pastoral staff should engage the person in conversation to determine their purpose and reason for being there. This is also a time when an evaluation can be made of the person's condition and intent.
- If it is determined that the person is agitated or disturbed, steps should be taken to de-escalate the situation. Calmly speak to the person in order to determine why he is there and what his needs are. By showing concern, you may be able to reason with the person to resolve any issues that are troubling to him.
- If it is safe to do so, accompany the person to a secluded office or classroom so as to talk to him to resolve the issues that caused him to come to the church. This will also remove the person from view of the congregation, thus avoiding any unnecessary disturbance.

At this point the situation has either been resolved safely or the decision for police intervention has been made.

In addition, there may be a situation when there is no immediate indication that a person is in the possession of a weapon. Think about this startling example. A young woman knelt at an altar before Sunday services at Love Center Ministries Church in Memphis, Tennessee, and asked the pastor to pray for her. He, as well as ten to fifteen other members of the church, prayed and told her the words, "The Lord loves you." After this, the woman walked to the back of the church and shot herself in the back of the skull. She had been a member of the church for seven years and was a counselor for troubled children. No one else was hurt in the incident.

It is impossible to provide specific guidelines to deal with every situation. Common sense, however, must prevail, and when in doubt you should contact your local law enforcement agency.

What to do when a menacing or dangerous intruder enters the church during office hours throughout the week

An unshaven, dirty man entered the Conway (Missouri) First Baptist Church and asked the pastor for some cash. Although the church didn't give cash when assisting people, they have a special fund used to pay for meals for the needy. As the pastor was on the telephone with a local restaurant owner, the intruder pushed him into a bookshelf and stabbed him three times with a knife. The intruder snatched the pastor's billfold and fled the church. The pastor suffered minor knife wounds to one of his hands, his abdomen, and leg, and was treated at a nearby hospital.

Here are the steps that should be followed in the event that a menacing or dangerous intruder enters your church during office hours throughout the week.

- Limit access to the building by having only one door, or as few doors as possible, where visitors must enter. This will allow each person who enters the building to be noticed by staff members. This is more difficult for large church structures that require multiple avenues of ingress and egress.
- A receptionist or other staff member should be located near the entrance in order to greet anyone who enters in order to engage them in conversation. This will allow all who enter to be known and the receptionist can evaluate the purpose of the person's visit. The receptionist or staff member should be placed behind a barrier such as some type of counter, desk, or wall to provide safety from an aggressive or dangerous person. It is also suggested that the receptionist have access to a telephone, intercom system, or other device that can be used to summon assistance in the event a dangerous intruder enters the church.
- If possible, the receptionist or staff member should be in a position to view the church parking lot in order to see anyone who may enter the church before they walk through the door. This may allow them to be alerted to a possible violent intruder and provide time to appropriately react.

- As addressed in chapter 4, a visitor processing and screening procedure that will screen all visitors as they enter the church should also be established.
- Give consideration to the inner and outer security perimeter of the church structure as discussed in chapter 4, regarding security issues for the church-owned day care, preschool, and elementary.
- Chapter 4 also suggests that at the location where visitor screening will occur, information on church adherents who may be involved in divorce proceedings, child custody disputes, and any other possible problems that may spill over to the church be provided.
- If your church utilizes closed circuit television surveillance cameras (as addressed in ch. 7), this system could be effectively utilized to monitor the whereabouts and behavior of an intruder without having direct contact. This would be very beneficial when reporting the actions of the intruder to the police.

What to do when a menacing or dangerous intruder is present on the church grounds but has not entered the building

If an intruder or threatening individual is encountered outside of the building(s) on church grounds, the staff member in charge of security must be notified immediately. At that point, decisions will be made regarding the appropriate action to take. If it is obvious that the intruder is armed with a weapon, the person who makes this observation should immediately call the police.

The following consists of actions that can be taken in the event an intruder or menacing person is on church grounds but has not entered the building.

- If the intruder has a weapon, immediately call 911 (if 911 service exists in your area).
- If at any time the person makes comments or displays behavior that indicates that he/she may be a danger to themselves or someone else, the police should be notified immediately.

- Instruct those who are outside to come into the nearest building.
- If safety permits, lock all exterior doors to prevent the intruder from entering the building(s).
- Direct anyone in a hallway or restroom to come into a secured room.
- If possible, close, lock, and cover all windows.
- Turn off all lights.
- No one should be allowed to leave any building while the intruder is still at large.
- A staff member or security team member will instruct anyone who is outside the building to move away from the threatening person.
- No one should be allowed to leave a secured classroom, office, or building until informed that it is safe to do so by the staff member in charge of security or the police.
- Lock exterior doors to all other buildings on the church grounds.
- Staff and members of the congregation in other buildings unaffected by the crisis (if your church facility has multiple buildings) should remain inside and sit quietly in locked classrooms and offices. Those who are outside at the time should be instructed to come inside the unaffected building.

If it is evident that the intruder does not have a weapon, the same plan of action addressed for the unarmed intruder who enters the church building can be applied.

Concluding Considerations

By using the previously established procedures, threats of these four different natures can be handled with the least endangerment to all concerned. However, circumstances may exist that may make it impossible to follow an established plan of action. People who are confronted by the intruder, faced with a particular situation by the intruder, or isolated in a particular section of the building may have to make very difficult decisions based on what they think is best for them. For example, the individual may have an available means of escape without being detected by the intruder, lock a door, lie on the floor to avoid detection and harm, call 911, or signal police from a window, while remaining out of the view of the intruder. Inasmuch as these measures may be risky with respect to the person's safety, they may be the only options available to save your life or the lives of others.

Churches have access to a wealth of knowledge and expertise in their local law enforcement agencies. Most police departments have crime prevention officers whose job is to provide security surveys to business entities and other groups in the community, including churches. They can make recommendations regarding security measures tailored to meet the security needs of your church. It is highly suggested that you contact your local law enforcement agency, fire department, or local government agencies to request their assistance in developing and implementing your security program. Additionally, my company, Robert Cirtin Investigations, provides consulting services to churches in this regard.

As a former police officer, I know that many churches have police officers in attendance during worship services. If a police officer is present when an incident of this nature occurs, he or she will take control of the situation and it will be the responsibility of the staff and congregation to follow his instruction. While the police officer is responding to the direct threat presented by the intruder, the church staff may also implement the plan of action.

I have the unique perspective of being a former police officer and having formerly participated in full-time church ministry. I understand that many church leaders and congregations would rather not think about the subject matter in this chapter or even this entire book. Nevertheless, our culture continues to change, and many of these vicissitudes contribute to the violent nature of some in our society. It has, therefore, become imperative that God's children seriously consider church safety and security.

Just as many churches have become proactive with regard to evangelism, worship, education, missions, and building projects,

40

churches must also become proactive instead of reactive regarding church safety and security. My hope is that church leaders and congregations will find a good balance of providing a nurturing, yet safe, environment in which people may come to worship God.

Chapter 3

Issues Relating To Child Physical And Sexual Abuse And Child Neglect

Donna M. Washburn, B.S.W., M.S.W., L.C.S.W. (Licensed Clinical Social Worker)

Child Abuse And The Church

Upon graduation from seminary, Pastor White had never envisioned his journey in the ministry to include police cars, criminal investigators, state social workers, media personnel, and distraught congregates, not to mention several children whose lives had been irrevocably and traumatically changed forever. However, this is exactly the scene he faced one cold, February morning, standing on the steps of his small, rural community church. A deep anxiety gripped his heart and a wave of physical dread spread to his stomach as the one question he knew, yet hoped would never come, was heralded by a local newspaper reporter. "Pastor, were you aware that youth sponsor Steven Smith was sexually molesting his daughter, and also several other female children of your congregation? And if so, why did you not contact the authorities?" And so began two years of equally difficult and morally convicting legal proceedings, which ultimately divided his church and devastated Pastor White's ministry.

The legal investigation concluded that the church had been grossly negligent in failing to protect the children in the church from Smith. A simple background check with the state's Child Abuse and Neglect Registry would have revealed that Smith had been investigated several years before in regard to allegations of inappropriate sexual contact with a minor. In addition, Pastor White and a staff member were found to be in violation of the state's child abuse mandatory reporting law. It was discovered that the staff member had approached Pastor White six months prior with

43

concerns stemming from a statement made by Smith's daughter on a field trip. Essentially, she (the daughter) had disclosed fear to return home because her father was there and would "want to spend special time with me in my bedroom, and that always hurts." Pastor White had evaluated this report and casually mentioned the incident to Smith with an offer of pastoral counseling if there were any "family problems." Smith laughed it off stating his daughter had watched too many of those "liberal after school specials." The subject was never broached again despite many physical and behavioral symptoms displayed by the young girl in subsequent months.

This case clearly illustrates the church's need for education surrounding child sexual abuse and specific procedures to prevent the occurrence of abuse within its walls. In addition, it demonstrates the need for established policies to deal with general suspicions of abuse, which may potentially occur externally, that is, in the homes of children of regular church attendants. This chapter will briefly discuss:

- current statistics on how the church is an institution struggling with this disturbing issue.
- basic symptoms of abused children.
- practical suggestions for basic policy procedures to safeguard the church and its congregates.

Thousands of churches around the United States could very easily be substituted for the story of Pastor Smith and his church. Pick up any newspaper, surf through a multitude of television news headlines on any given day and one is bound to find a story of sexual abuse scandals in the Catholic church. However, the Protestant church should not be lulled into a state of complacent denial of child abuse occurring within its walls. According to Clayton, 2002, the Catholic churches make up only five percent of the 350,000 churches in the United States, and since 1993, there have been over 3,500 allegations annually in the Protestant church. It seems that there is often a cloak of secrecy surrounding sexual and physical abuse issues in the church, or at the very least the philosophy that these issues should be dealt with internally. Therefore, abuse statistics are likely even higher than are currently reported. The other common myth is that if abuse really does occur within the realm of the church, it is perpetrated by the clergy. The reality is in a recent study, 42 percent of alleged child abusers in the context of the church were volunteers, 25 percent were paid staff and clergy, and 25 percent were other children (Clayton, 2002).

While child abuse within the internal workings of a church setting often prompts immediate church action, and some churches outline policies to protect against it, often forgotten are the children in attendance who experience abuse in their homes, yet return Sunday after Sunday without any intervention in their lives. Often, people of Christian faith believe that child abuse is a secular sin, and is not something that the church plays any role in detecting. The truth is that in the year 2002, 896,000 children were confirmed victims of maltreatment including physical, sexual, emotional abuse, and neglect. (National Clearinghouse on Child Abuse and Neglect information)

According to recent (2003) research on religious affiliation and church attendance in the United States, 43 percent of American adults attend church in a typical weekend (Barna Research Online). With this statistic in mind, it would be remiss for the church to assume victims of child abuse are not in attendance. This is especially true for churches utilizing a bus ministry, or who have an extensive children's program, as the statistics usually increase with these populations. Additionally, most researchers and experts in the field of sexual abuse stipulate that on average, 1 in 4 girls and 1 in 9 boys will experience some form of sexual abuse during their childhood. Once again, with a statistic of this significance, it is a certainty that the church will without a doubt come into contact with children who have been, or who are currently experiencing some form of abuse. Furthermore, many incestuous families adhere to strong patriarchal and often religious tenets despite how dysfunctional they might be. Therefore, it is quite possible (and in all reality very probable) that there are members in a multitude of churches grappling in secrecy with sexual abuse in their homes, all the while attending church and worshiping next to others. Finally, mere statistics dictate that with the sheer number of citizens attending churches in the United States, abuse will occur *to* members of their congregations, and often *by* members of their congregation. It is overwhelmingly important, then, for church leadership to be educated on issues of child abuse, have policies and procedures established to deal with such an issue, and develop safeguards against abuse in the church.

On being presented with the argument above, many church leaders will agree that further steps must be taken in their church to address this issue. However, many then ask, "What are these steps and how does a church implement them?" The remainder of this chapter will focus on these questions and strive to provide answers and basic guidelines that any congregation can follow.

Preventing Abuse From Occurring Within The Walls Of The Church

One of the best ways of dealing with abuse in the church is preventing it from happening in the first place. While this may seem simplistic in nature, there are tried and true methods of safety and policy that can protect children and congregants from those wanting to bring harm to them. While church leaders cannot say with 100 percent certainty that they can eliminate all variables that often breed abuse, following the guidelines below vastly increases this likelihood.

1. Educating The Church On Issues Of Child Physical And Sexual Abuse

It has been said that information is power, and this topic is by no means an exception to this belief. Research and anecdotal evidence has shown that when those living and interacting with victims of abuse were interviewed regarding their knowledge of the situation, common themes of "I didn't realize what was happening," or "I thought he (the perpetrator) was just a really nice guy who had a heart for children" constantly reoccurred. In further support, this author has found that after many years of teaching in the university setting, the majority of young adults do not have even the most basic understanding of abuse characteristics and statistics. This would suggest that many in a church congregation lack this information as well. So why is it so important that they are educated? Simply for the fact that this education can lead to early intervention, and even prevention of potential sexual or physical abuse. Church workers are unable to intervene in abusive situations or even identify them without the proper training and education. Should leadership choose to provide this training there are a variety of methods and formats that can be adopted.

Training facilitated by experts in the field of child abuse

It is important that those providing this sensitive training are up to date on the latest research and trends in the field. As horrifying as it is, this field is growing yearly and new studies are constantly revealing additional pertinent information. There are a variety of sources to turn to for this knowledge.

State authority for the protection of children and families

Often they are known as "The Division of Family Services," or "Division of Child Protective Services," or occasionally lumped under "The Division of Human Services." Whatever the title might be for each given state, there are mandatory state agencies developed precisely for dealing with issues of abuse in the home. Contacting the local Family Services office and forming a positive relationship with its staff is vital in the church's proactive stance to this issue. Requesting one of their social workers or educators to do a one-day training at a local church is usually welcomed and provided.

A trained consultant

There are various professionals across the nation, such as the author of this chapter, that will contract to serve as a consultant to the church. This service can range from simple education to complete development of policies and procedures, including forms specific to the church and the state it is located in.

Victim's center or child advocacy center

Many counties throughout the United States have centers developed solely for the purpose of assisting victims of violence or sexual crimes. Often they are specialized in working with children, and not only provide treatment but also are passionate about educating the community on the evils of abuse. Once again, requesting a social worker or educator will likely be received positively and a training course readily developed.

Colleges and universities

Should a church be located near a college or university, a professional may be found within these communities to provide training, especially if these institutions have degree programs in the Behavioral Science fields. Additional fields may include Human Services, Counseling, and Early Childhood Education. Often it is in this arena that current research may be accessed and can be included in any training given.

Local professionals

Should none of the above services be available, church leadership should seek out a local professional working in the field. This service may be found in one of the local school counselors, psychologists, or social workers. Additionally, many mental health counselors or therapists have received competent training in child abuse issues. One should be cautious however, to ascertain the professional's educational background. In order to ensure the information is consistent with general research and study, it is wise to limit the use of professionals to those with a state sanctioned license. Often this requires a master's degree in a field such as social work or counseling, and often carry titles such as but are not limited to: Licensed Clinical Social Worker, Licensed Practical Counselor, or Certified Counselor.

Seminars or workshop facilitators

Should a church find itself in the unique position that it is unable to find any local professionals to conduct training, regional seminars or workshops are often available throughout the year in larger cities. While this may be more costly than the other alternatives, it may be feasible for the church leadership or staff to attend, and bring back the information for the rest of the congregation or volunteer workers. These workshops may be found through the state agencies discussed above, internet searches, or by contacting state universities involved in community education.

Once an educational resource has been identified, churches must then determine who will be in attendance of such training. It is strongly suggested that all staff and volunteers who interact with children on any level receive the training, and all "leadership" staff including pastors, youth pastors, children's pastors, and Sunday school coordinators. Furthermore, it is suggested that these, and any others in positions of authority, receive a supplemental session to discuss administrative issues such as policies and procedures (to be identified later in this chapter).

Some churches may wish to open this training up to all members of the congregation simply as further knowledge for their own families. While this goes to community support and solidifying the church's stance on abuse, it should not (and in all reality, *cannot*) be mandated.

Note: It is always a good practice to look within the walls of the church for these professionals. Many churches have congregants or even staff members who carry such professional licenses and thus would be aware of the unique needs and characteristics of the congregation.

2. Screen All Workers

While screening of workers is often a controversial and sometimes resisted practice, it is essential in the protection of children. The nature of most churches is one of family ties and close community bonds. This leads many into a false sense of security that all members are upstanding citizens incapable of participating or initiating abusive acts. Sadly, as shown in the statistics discussed in the beginning of this chapter, this is not always true. Perpetrators of abuse are smart enough to seek out vulnerable and trusting congregations to prey upon. It is here that a simple screening of the worker may produce a negative history that would preclude the worker from having access to children. In the example at the beginning of this chapter, this type of screening would have easily prevented the destruction that was brought into so many lives. Screening should at a minimum include the following:

Basic screening form or application
- All identifying information of the potential volunteer including current and past addresses (for a minimum of a five- to seven-year period)
- Social Security number
- Criminal history
- A question which asks if this individual has ever had an allegation of sexual or physical abuse brought against them, and a thorough explanation of this occurrence
- Experience the individual has had with children, including work in past churches
- Areas in which this individual is interested in working
- Two or three personal and previous church references — these must be called and verified by a staff member of the church

Following completion of the basic screening form or application, a criminal background check must be performed.

Criminal background check
Criminal background screenings are essential in detecting any previous criminal behavior that has not been reported by the individual. Screenings may be conducted in two manners. The first option that the church has is to conduct the screening itself using state criminal background screening forms. They are state regulated and often may be downloaded directly from the state government website. Should that not be available, forms can be requested by mail. Once filled in by the individual, they are sent to the state for processing and then any information obtained is mailed directly to church staff. Often there is a minimal fee for this processing. The other option a church has is to hire an investigation

firm who provides pre-employment screening services. (See ch. 1 for more information on background screening.)

Please note that simply requesting a criminal background check is often not enough.

Child abuse/neglect screening

Many states have a separate reporting agency for the detection and investigation of child abuse. It is very possible that someone has been accused of sexually abusing a child and has been investigated by the state, however no criminal charges have been filed. In this instance, the criminal background check would return clear. Therefore, it is *essential* that churches request the state to screen for child abuse and neglect reports. Again, in many states these forms may also be downloaded from the Internet or requested from the State Division of Family Services. Often, this process has been streamlined into one form and a church is at liberty to check off the types of screenings they desire.

Removal of individuals with negative results on their background checks

While most churches operate under biblical principles of forgiveness and grace, it is crucial that individuals with a past criminal history, or abuse allegations or convictions, be removed from consideration in working with children. They should be counseled into other forms of service in the church, and should not be ostracized from the church. However, they cannot work with children. Not only is this to protect the children and the church, but also to protect the individual. Placing even a reformed abuser in a children's program immediately opens them up to suspicion and potential false allegations.

Personal interview

Once an individual has had a clear background result, it is recommended they have a personal interview with church leadership. The senior pastor, or another leader in charge of children's programs, may conduct this interview. Types of questions asked may include: description of why they want to work with children, any past issues that may be relevant such as a history of being a victim of abuse, and their philosophy of discipline. It is during this interview that the individual can be made aware of all church policies and procedures related to working with children.

3. Place Importance On Children's Programs

Too many times, children's programs in the realm of the church are neglected and the last to be considered when discussing budgeting, staffing, and even housing concerns. This sets up a general attitude that these programs are of little importance to the functioning of the church. In turn, this can be construed as a lack of the importance of children. Therefore, churches should make a concerted effort to enhance the overall attitude and attention given to children's programs. This can be done by having a periodic "Children's Sunday"; coordinating work days to improve the conditions of the nurseries, classrooms, and activity centers; throwing a "nursery shower" for needed provisions in the nurseries and toddler areas; increasing budgetary allowances for children's programs; and appointing a staff member to oversee and coordinate all children's programs.

4. Building And Remodeling Safe Facilities

As discussed in point 3 above, children's programs are often neglected in the construction of churches, especially smaller churches that grow quickly. Space issues often require otherwise inappropriate areas to be turned into Sunday school rooms or nursery areas. The results can be disastrous and set up a potentially abusive situation. The following guidelines are helpful to prevent opportunities for adults to take advantage of children.

- Allow visual access into all rooms occupied by children either by inserting windows into all classroom doors or replacing the doors with those that are glass or have large windows already built in.
- Avoid placing nurseries and classrooms in a basement area or any other type of physically isolated rooms that are far from the general congregation.

- Should children's facilities be isolated from the general congregation, post security personnel or staff members in various locations throughout the services to serve as monitors. (See ch. 6 pertaining to establishing a church security officer program.)
- Nurseries and toddler rooms should have a large glass window for those passing by to easily see their children.
- Churches with the financial abilities should place security cameras in all locations where children's programs are conducted or places that are frequented by children such as hallways and playgrounds. (See ch. 7 pertaining to the utilization of surveillance/security cameras.)

5. Supervisory Policies

Two adults at all times

Workers should never be alone with children, even if they are of the same gender. There should always be two adults present, and preferably two adults of the opposite gender. No one should work in the nursery or preschool area alone, even if they have their own children with them. This also applies to older child programs and even youth groups. Any, and all, programs dealing with children under eighteen years of age should follow this policy. In addition, workers should never take children to restroom facilities alone, and never should assist children of the opposite gender. Not only does this protect the children, but also protects the worker from false allegations.

Not from the same family

Do not let teams of workers from the same family work together without another person in the room. While this is chilling to think about, family members sometimes collude together to victimize children. This prevents this situation.

Follow the six-month rule

All workers must be faithful attendees of the church for at least six months prior to beginning work in a children's program.

This is sometimes difficult due to the desperate need for workers, however many church leaders have wished they had come to know individuals prior to allowing them to work in their programs.

Use a nursery and/or preschool identification procedure

All children should be numbered or some other way paired with their guardian. Parents or guardians must then present the proper identifying article in order to retrieve their child. An example would be randomly numbering children as they are checked into the program, and giving the parent or guardian some physical representation of that number (such as a ticket or laminated card). The child is tagged with the corresponding number. This may be safely done with a safety pin, clip, or badge that attaches to the child's clothing. Parents must then present the ticket or badge to nursery workers at the end of the service. This policy prevents anyone but the parent from removing a child from the nursery. In some larger congregations, leadership has included the policy of having parents register their child in the program prior to regular attendance, and then having them provide appropriate identification when retrieving their child.

When calling a parent out of service

Should nursery workers need to call a parent to come retrieve their child, an usher or deacon should be used. Nursery workers should never leave their appointed site, thus rendering their partner alone with children. Many churches have electronic means of calling parents out of a service using their child's assigned number. These churches have digital numeric displays located in the sanctuary/worship center easily visible to all parents. Nursery or preschool workers have access to a control pad and can manually punch in the child's number that corresponds to the parent needed. This option is relatively inexpensive and nursery workers have testified that it is a great time saver, safety feature, and needed device.

Assigned nursery workers

Allow only assigned workers or their approved substitutes into the nursery. Again, this is difficult when working with volunteer staff, as many weekends there is a lack of workers due to illness, vacation, or simply a lack of responsibility. This is where a good children's coordinator will have an extensive listing of approved substitutes. All of these substitutes must have been screened and gone through all appropriate checks and interviews prior to their time to work.

Continual supervision

Do not permit any child to be unsupervised or leave the program at any time without their parent or guardian. It is these situations where youth often become victims of older members in the children's program. Workers should never allow an older child to have responsibility for a younger child, even in the context of teen programs. For this purpose, it is wise to stipulate that no worker be under the age of eighteen, or at least sixteen with the supervision of an adult.

Obtain parental consent before taking a child anywhere

Permission forms must be obtained before any outings or field trips take place. Again, there must be two or more adults of different genders supervising these outings.

Monitor all programs

Ushers, church security personnel, or other specified church leaders should randomly and periodically pass by and view programs in progress. During a typical Sunday service, these individuals should simply visually inspect all of the various nurseries, children's programs, and toddler rooms, to verify that no suspicious behavior is taking place. This can serve as a deterrent to anyone who may be lingering in children's areas or actively seeking out a child.

Develop a handbook

Regardless of the policies churches choose to adopt; placing them in an accessible handbook is important for consistency. All workers should have a copy or at least access to the handbook at all times, and staff must be trained in their specifics.

Obtain an agreement to follow policies

Lastly, all workers must indicate that they understand and agree to the church policies and signify this in writing and by their signatures.

Dealing With Abuse Once It Is Detected

As illustrated in the beginning of the chapter, child abuse has, and will, continue to surface in the modern church. How the church deals with this information has varied in the past, but this has now become a legal issue as well as a moral mandate.

Mandated reporters

In the majority of states, many church officials fail to recognize that under the Child Abuse Prevention and Treatment and Adoption Act of 1996 (CAPTA), pastors, lay leaders, and all church volunteers working with children are considered "Mandated Reporters." This means that by law they are required to report any suspicions of child abuse to the state social service department for further investigation. Failure to follow this law, resulting in the continuation of abuse, may result in fines at a minimum of $2,500 and two years in jail. These ramifications vary from state to state, and some states have fines in excess of $6,000, and jail sentences of three to five years. Many pastors and church leaders are lulled into thinking this law does not apply to them due to clergy/parishioner confidentiality laws, but this is not so in most cases. In most states this only is the case when the pastor obtains knowledge of child abuse through a "confessional" method such as counseling. However, the majority of the time it will be Sunday school workers, nursery workers, or staff members that become aware of the abuse. In these cases the worker, and in turn the church, is legally responsible to report the suspicion, and they are not covered by the same cloak of secrecy as the pastor. In the example at the beginning of the chapter, Pastor White did not learn of the abuse through counseling, but through a staff member. Therefore, he, the staff member, and the church as a whole were liable for not reporting the abuse. It is important that churches contact their State Department of Social Services, or a legal authority to determine specific laws pertaining to them.

Policies for dealing with abuse/determining when to report

Many well-intentioned individuals fail to report potential abuse due to the fact that they feel they do not have enough evidence. It must be made clear to all workers/staff/volunteers, that it is not their job to investigate suspicious behavior, but simply report it and let the experts and authorities follow-up with the child and individuals involved. Another common fear is that an individual who reports abuse may later be prosecuted for filing the report. This should not be a concern due to the fact that CAPTA requires states to enact legislation that provides for immunity from prosecution arising out of reporting abuse or neglect. Therefore, a person who reports abuse in "good faith" is absolutely immune from criminal and civil liability. This being said, any suspicious behavior that may indicate abuse occurring either within the walls of the church or to a child being victimized at home must be reported to the state authorities. This is where the training and education regarding signs and characteristics of abuse is essential. Workers cannot report abuse if they don't know what it looks like, or the type of behaviors an abused child may exhibit. Each state has a "hotline" number that immediately connects the caller with a trained state worker who will take the report, and then dispatch it to the local protective service unit. While each state hotline number is different, churches may call 1-800-4-A-CHILD or go to http://www.kidsafe-caps.org/report.html for a listing of all states and their hotline numbers. From there it is no longer the responsibility of the individual or the church, but the state, to determine if indeed abuse is occurring.

Developing a "plan" within an administrative framework

Each church must determine how to address a worker's concern regarding potential abuse. Here are some of the best ways to handle it.

- Develop a simple reporting form for workers to fill out should they feel it is deemed necessary.
- This form then can be turned into the coordinator of children's programs, who in turn consults with the pastor or designated staff member.
- At this point, the hotline telephone call should be made by the worker, but under the support and supervision of the pastor, designated staff member, or coordinator. It is recommended that the hotline call be placed within 24 hours of the initial concern. When placing a hotline call, the church should have certain information available, if possible. This includes: the child's full name, his/her parent's names, their current address(es), age, and a detailed explanation for the concern including where the abuse likely occurred and by whom. However, if the church does not have all of the above information, many hotlines will still take the report as long as the state workers can locate the child in question.
- Many states require that the individual who witnessed the concern or has the firsthand information must make the hotline call, however some states allow a church representative to register the report (contacting the state's hotline number and determining the state's preference when setting up this policy is advisable). It is important to note that the hotline call must be made as soon as possible, and should occur regardless of whom the "offending" party may be. This may become difficult when the allegations are against a longstanding member of the congregation, or perhaps a staff member.
- Workers should be instructed that simply filling out a church reporting form is not enough to fulfill their responsibility. They must place the hotline call themselves or

58

witness the call being made firsthand. The church reporting form is simply an accountable means of keeping all children's staff and church leadership aware of issues in the church, as well as thoroughly documenting the churches actions.

Removal of alleged offender

In the event that the abuse allegations are against a worker in the children's program, this person must be temporarily suspended from their duties pending the state's investigation. Not only does this potentially protect the child or children in question, but also protects the church from possible civil liability and even criminal charges. While this action is essential, it must be handled with the utmost sensitivity. It is neither the church's role nor competence to determine the alleged offenders guilt or innocence, and this should be clearly stated to the individual being suspended. It should be expressed as a matter of policy, and should the authorities deem the report as unsubstantiated, the member may once again be considered for children's work. This becomes a much easier task if this policy was clearly identified to the individual upon their commencement into the volunteer program of the church.

Providing support

Once a hotline call has been placed, the church must step back into its primary role in the community: the role of support and spiritual guidance. The victim, the victim's family, the offender, and many others involved will need ongoing emotional support and guidance. It is wise to identify trusted counselors in the community to refer to. Leadership in the church must guard against congregants ostracizing the victim, especially when the allegation is against an upstanding member of the church. It also should be determined what the stance of the leadership will be toward the offending party. All can be done within biblical context and support.

Basic Indicators Of Physical
And Sexual Child Abuse

This author was very hesitant to provide this section in the chapter due to the fact that a few lists of indicators in no way eliminates the need for a formal educational seminar or training in this subject. It is hoped that individuals reading this section will recognize the complexity of the topic, and this will stimulate a desire to gain further training and education. Any injury discovered should be evaluated using some of the characteristics addressed below, and if the child is verbal they should be gently questioned as to the cause of the injury. It should be noted that almost all of these indicators can be caused in some accidental occurrence, but concern should be noted when the injuries are *frequent*, occur in *patterns*, or are *inconsistent* with the child's or parent's story. There are some injuries that should never be present on a child; these are highlighted in the lists below. As discussed earlier in this chapter, any and all suspicious injuries should be "hotlined" immediately to the state reporting agency, and left for investigation by the experts.

Physical indicators of physical abuse
The most commonly identified and easily visual forms of abuse can often be seen on the body of an abused child.

Bruises
Having multiple bruises, or bruises in unlikely locations, may be a red flag that requires further investigation. This can be difficult as children often obtain multiple bruises naturally, simply due to their nature of play. However, it should be realized that bruises occurring after a fall or bicycle accident are going to be found on a child's bony extremities out of a defensive posture (such as on their elbows, knees, shins, or the palms of their hands). Therefore, a note should be made if bruises are seen in the following manners:

- In the "soft tissue" areas of the body such as the stomach, lower back, neck, or cheek
- On the interior of extremities such as inner arms, inner thighs, and side of the waist. These are often indicative of abusive types of grabs and holds
- Bruises that are in the form of an *object* such as a belt mark, hanger mark, extension cord, or hand print (these are all common forms of abuse that this researcher and others in the field have seen repeatedly)
- Multiple bruises in unusual patterns
- Bruises in clusters or located on one area of the child
- *Any* bruises on infants who are not yet mobile should present an immediate concern, as they are not typically capable of having accidental injuries
- Multiple bruises in various stages of healing (more recent bruises are darker and may have a blue or black tint, and will turn yellow and brown as they age). It often will take five to seven days for a bruise to disappear, and more severe bruises can take up to two weeks to heal. This information is helpful when determining if the "story" given for the bruise is consistent with the time frame of the bodily evidence

Lacerations/abrasions/and other injuries

More severe types of abuse can result in actual puncture wounds or lacerations to a child's body. These again should be evaluated in the context of the child's age and their explanation of the injury. The following should be noted for concern:

- Cuts or wounds on the eyes, lips, face, or ears
- Lacerations or "digs" on a child's arm or other body part indicating fingernail penetration
- Bumps or lumps on a child's skull, especially if they occur often or in multiple areas
- Patches of hair loss indicating possible hair pulling
- *Any* injuries on the genitals of a child not consistent with diaper rash (these might be seen when diapering an infant or non-toilet trained toddler)

61

- *Any* blood in a child's underwear or diaper should immediately be investigated

Fractures or broken bones

While it is true that children seem to be accident prone due to their lack of coordination and rapidly growing bodies, there can be red flags when a child has certain characteristics or patterns of broken bones, such as:

- Fractures or breaks in the long bones (arms and legs) which are frequent or are accompanied by bruising
- Spiral fractures caused by twisting of an extremity
- Broken ribs (it is very rare that a child of any age have an accident outside of an automobile that results in broken or fractured ribs)
- Skull fractures not otherwise explained
- *Any* fracture in an infant who is non-mobile
- Concern should be noted when there is an inconsistency in a child's or parent's story regarding the cause of the fracture

Burns

Some of the most horrific and disturbing cases of abuse involve the use of burns. While some burns occur accidentally, they are not common and should be investigated immediately. Accidental burns take an irregular shape as the child quickly removes the body part or jumps away. Intentional burns are often very symmetrical and regular in shape, and should raise a red flag. The following identifies burns that should be evaluated immediately:

- Immersion burns — look as though the child was placed in hot or scalding water and held there. Often referred to as "doughnut shaped" as the buttocks are often scaled around the edges and middle of the flesh, and not on the bottom where the child was held down
- Circular shaped burns resulting from cigarettes, lighters, or other heated objects

- Stocking burns — so-called because of a distinct pattern of burning over a child's foot or hand, and immediately stopping just above the ankle or wrist indicating the child was forcibly restrained
- Burns which resemble an object such as a curling iron or clothes iron
- *Any* burns found on a non-mobile infant should immediately be hotlined

Behavioral indicators of physical abuse

Often children will not only exhibit physical signs they are being battered, but will display behavioral indications that can be evaluated in conjunction with physical evidence. The following should be considered when evaluating an injury:

- Avoids physical contact with adults
- Cries easily when spoken to sternly
- Winces or shrinks back when an adult attempts to touch or hug them
- Wears clothing inappropriate for the weather (i.e. long pants and a sweat shirt on a warm summer day)
- Exhibits fear of adults, possibly one gender over the other
- May stay isolated from other children
- May be overly aggressive (from learning this behavior in his/her own home)
- Complains of pains or aches regularly
- Inconsistent story of the cause of injury
- Fearful of parental involvement in discussion of injury

Physical indicators of child sexual abuse

The most disturbing and often incomprehensible form of child abuse is the sexual use of their bodies by an adult or older child. Statistics show that up to eighty percent of victims knew their perpetrator, and as high at sixty percent of all abuse occurs at the hands of a family member. This type of abuse is often very difficult to detect visually, and there may be little to no physical indicators. Behavioral indicators or verbal disclosures are usually the indicators present, though there may be physical indicators as discussed below:

- Bruises or bleeding in the genital area (may be the result of physical abuse or sexual abuse)
- Complains of pain in the genital area
- Refuses to urinate or pain during urination
- Difficulty walking or sitting
- Cries excessively during diaper changes as a result of pain
- Touches themselves or other children in sexual ways (while it is normal for children to "experiment" or be curious during childhood regarding sexual matters, they often are not persistent with such play or do not have sophisticated knowledge of sexual acts)
- Attempts to touch adult workers in a sexual fashion
- Torn or bloodied underwear
- *Any* sexually transmitted disease should immediately be hotlined
- Bedwetting or urinating in their clothing during the day of an otherwise toilet-trained child is considered a red flag in this field

Behavioral indicators of child sexual abuse

As discussed above, behavioral indicators are often more common and present in greater number than physical signs. They include:

- Excessive discussion of sexual matters
- Fear of adults, specifically one gender over the other
- Seductive behavior or exposing their genitals to others
- Sexual drawings or artwork
- Fire starting (another major red flag in the field of sexual abuse)
- Excessive stomachaches or headaches (anxiety related)
- Depression
- Withdrawn and isolated

- Low self-esteem
- Altered sleep patterns or nightmares

In older children or teens:

- Sexual promiscuity
- Alcohol or drug use
- Excessive flirtation or seduction with adults or other teens

Family or parental indicators of child physical and sexual abuse
It is often said that a child's display of physical or behavioral cues of abuse are just symptoms of family dysfunction. Children are not trained as well as adults to mask their pain and anguish, and this is often where professionals find their clues for family problems. This being said, there are certain family or parental characteristics that can be considered in conjunction with the child's physical or behavioral indicators, all adding up to a picture of abuse. Some of the most common are:

- Multiple personal problems of one or both of the parents
- Marital problems
- Violence in the marriage
- Parents raised in abusive families of origin
- Highly authoritarian or rigid parenting style by one or both of the parents
- Excessive control or domination of the father over the mother and children
- Isolation of the family, either in physical location of their home or lack of participation in any activities, outings, or entertainment
- Easily agitated or hard to please in any setting or program
- Does not demonstrate affection or concern for their child
- Explanation for injuries is inconsistent with physical evidence
- Evasive or uncooperative when questioned about child's injuries

- Blames child for all injuries
- Becomes extremely agitated or aggressive when questioned
- Criticizes or calls the child names

It must be reiterated that any of the above physical, behavioral, or parental indicators in isolation could be attributed to any number of explanations. Therefore, it is often the pattern of or shear multitude of indicators that lead caregivers to suspect abuse. As stated at the beginning of this section, it is this author's belief that simply reading these lists does not provide enough training, and it is strongly recommended that churches seek out a professional to conduct a seminar on this topic.

Conclusion

It has been shown that child abuse is a very real and pervasive concern in today's church. Church leaders must take action to protect the very lives that have been entrusted to them, and in turn protect their church and workers. This chapter has illustrated practical policies and guidelines to enact in church programs, and additional resources can be found on the reference list at the end of this chapter. It should be noted that the illustrative example that opened this chapter was based on a real church and real events. Names have been changed to protect those involved.

References And Additional Resources

References

Anderson, B. (1992). *When Child Abuse Comes to Church*. Bethany House Publishers; Minneapolis, Minnesota.

Barna Group On-line. (2003) "America's Faith *Is* Changing — But Beneath the Surface."
http:\\www.barna.org\FlexPage.aspx?Page+BarnaUpdate&Barna UpdateID=135.

Clayton, M. (2002). "Sex Abuse Spans Spectrum of Churches" in *Christian Science Monitor*.
www.csmonitor.com/2002/0405/p01s01-ussc.html.

Crosson-Tower, C. (2005) *Understanding Child Abuse and Neglect*, 6th ed., Allyn & Bacon: Boston, Massachusetts.

For Kids' Sake. (1998). *Investigating Child Abuse*. R. C. Law & Co., Inc., Chino, California.

Hammar, R. R., Klipowicz, S. W., & Cobble, J. F. (1993). *Church Law and Tax Report: Reducing the Risk of Child Sexual Abuse in Your Church — A complete and practical guidebook for prevention and risk*. Christian Ministries Resources: Matthews, North Carolina.

Heggen, C. H. (1993). *Sexual Abuse in Christian Homes and Churches*. Herald Press: Scottsdale, Arizona.

Internet References and Resources

Child Safety Institute — Child Abuse Prevention Series (CAPS)
http:\\www.kidsafe-caps.org/.

"Mandatory Reporting of Child Abuse and Neglect" by Susan K. Smith, Attorney at Law, Hartford & Avon, Connecticut.
http:\\www.smith-lawform.com.mandatory_reporting.htm.

National Clearinghouse on Child Abuse and Neglect information
http:\\nccanch.acf.hhs.gov/index.cfm.

Chapter 4

Safety And Security Issues For The Church-owned Day Care, Preschool, And Christian School

Dennis K. Lewis, M.S., B.S.

Trisha was in her third week of part-time employment for the local church day care center and found working around young children to be rewarding, as well as an opportunity to prepare for a future career as an elementary school teacher. The day care center had been in business for nine years and had an average daily attendance of 55 children. Most of the children were in attendance five days each week and all were between two and five years of age.

At approximately 1:30 p.m. Trisha answered the telephone and was informed that the caller was a "Mrs. Tuttle." The caller stated that she would be picking up her five-year-old daughter early for a doctor's appointment that afternoon. At 2 p.m. a woman in her thirties arrived at the center, identified herself as Brittany's mother, and stated that she was there to pick up her daughter, Brittany Tuttle, for a doctor's appointment. Trisha called the five-year-old classroom on the intercom and asked that Brittany report to the office because her mother was there to pick her up. Due to the fact that Brittany's teacher was alone in the classroom and could not leave the others unattended, she directed Brittany to "walk to office and see Trisha at the desk."

Within a few minutes, Trisha heard Brittany walking down the hall. As Brittany came into view, "Mrs. Tuttle" called her by name and said she was there to pick her up. Trisha observed Brittany smile and run into the arms of the woman and receive a kiss. "Mrs. Tuttle" then told Brittany that they needed to leave immediately, took her by the hand, and started toward the door. It was then that Trisha remembered she was supposed to have parents sign their children in and out on a form in the office when they were picking them up prior to the pre-designated time. Trisha informed "Mrs. Tuttle" that she needed to sign Brittany out. Trisha thought to herself that the woman was unfriendly and acting a bit nervous. It also surprised Trisha that the woman did not seem familiar with the routine office procedure. As the woman left with Brittany, Trisha noticed that her handwriting was almost illegible.

At 4:30 p.m. that same day, Trisha was finishing her working routine. Most of the children were gone, and she had returned to the classroom to help the one remaining teacher entertain the children. Shortly before 5 p.m., a gentleman that Trisha immediately recognized as Brittany Tuttle's father arrived at the classroom door and stated that he was there to pick up his daughter. At that time, Trisha informed him that his wife had already picked up Brittany and taken her to doctor's appointment. Mr. Tuttle immediately looked startled and appeared frightened. He then told Trisha that his wife was currently with him and had not picked Brittany up earlier in the day.

Without saying anything further, Mr. Tuttle told Trisha to call the police because, "Brittany has probably been abducted by her natural mother." He also stated that the ex-wife had no custody or visitation rights.

Trisha immediately called the police, while attempting to calm Mr. Tuttle. Mr. Tuttle began to berate Trisha for "not checking the enrollment information" that would have indicated that the natural mother was not to have any contact with Brittany. As the stepmother entered the classroom, Trisha could immediately see that this was not the same woman that had picked up Brittany earlier in the day.

The police arrived a short time later and began the investigation. Trisha was extremely distraught and had a difficult time answering their questions. Ultimately, the police were able to gather a physical description of "Mrs. Tuttle," along with a partial vehicle description.

"Mrs. Tuttle" was later stopped by the highway patrol for speeding about 100 miles from the day care center. A routine check of her driver's license indicated that the motorist's name was Janet Young, a suspect wanted for child abduction. Ms. Young was taken into custody and, several hours later, Brittany was reunited with her dad.

This illustration serves as a cogent example of the many issues facing the church-owned day care, preschool, and Christian school.

The process of establishing basic security functions for any organization that is charged with the education and/or care of children requires one to understand and estimate the threat, as well as determine the will and commitment of those that ultimately have to fund and defend the process. Institutions such as schools, both private and public, churches, shopping malls, and recreation centers are among those that create extreme difficulty because of the expectation by the public that access remain open while personal well-being is assured.

It is critical to understand that an individual that is persistent in the desire to inflict harm upon others is difficult to deter or stop, even with the most stringent of security in place. For those charged with developing security, simply delaying the perpetrator(s), or minimizing the damage may be the best outcome once the individual's actions have begun.

Comprehensive Security Planning

Access control

In order to determine how to implement access control methods, one has to identify the location of the inner and outer security perimeter. For most institutions where children are educated or cared for, the outer perimeter will encompass two specific areas, usually a playground or exercise area and the entry points to the actual facility where the children are housed.

When constructing a recreation or playground area, it is recommended that it be located in such a way that, should a threat emerge from the parking lot or street, children could be ushered back into the facility in less time than the threat could reasonably reach them. When combined with alert supervision, this provides the best strategy for sheltering children should a threat develop when they are at play.

The use of a "barrier" will provide further security to children in a play or recreation area. Fencing is the most common type of barrier used and should be at least five feet in height. Chain-link fence or other material that allows supervisors to view beyond the barrier is recommended. When using solid board fencing, the ability of adults to recognize a threat early is significantly reduced. Landscaping can be used to create a secondary barrier. Utilizing hedgerows or other foliage interconnected away from, and parallel to, the fence can provide further deterrence and increase the alert time when a threat is present. It is important to keep foliage used as a secondary barrier to a height that does not exceed three feet to keep it from being utilized as a place of concealment.

Access from parking lots or streets to play areas should not be encouraged, and walking paths should not be conveniently accessible to the parking lot and/or street. While they may ultimately lead to those locations, easy access simply decreases the time one might have to observe an approaching threat. The use of meandering walks is an excellent strategy. This is due to the fact that an aggressive or agitated person may disregard the designated walking path and traverse directly to the gate or to the target making the perpetrator more easily noticed.

The second outer perimeter is the exterior of the building. Many existing facilities were not constructed with security as a top priority, thus there may be multiple points of entry. The use of clearly stated and visibly posted signs in advance of arriving at the building is recommended. Signs should clearly identify parking areas and the main point of entry to the building. Individuals that do not pose a threat will usually comply with posted directions, while those coming for less than legitimate purposes will oftentimes vary from the instructions. Those that vary should be monitored to determine their intentions.

As much as is practical, the number of entry locations for visitors should be kept to a minimum. It is recommended that entry points be in view of office staff or other adult supervision. Signs should direct persons entering the facility to proceed to a designated location. It is also preferable that the parking lot be viewed from the office or other locations in the facility where adults generally are present.

For evening and nighttime security, all exterior doorways should be brightly illuminated. Parking lots should be well lit, and employees who work during this period should park where it is the shortest walking distance from the building to their vehicles.

Foliage at or near the building should conform to the three-seven rule. Bushes and other landscaping plants should not exceed a height of three feet. Trees should have all limbs and foliage trimmed from the ground up to seven feet. At least once a year, a "walk around" should be conducted at night to ensure that growth of foliage during the past year is not impacting security lighting by creating areas of shadow. By being selective in what is planted, and with proper trimming, areas of potential concealment can be eliminated.

The last important aspect of access control is the inner perimeter. The inner perimeter is the central office area and those places where children are present within the facility. It is not just the physical barriers, such as doors, created within the facility that form a security barrier, but it is also the actual adults working within.

While no two organizations will have identical designs, they usually fall into one of two categories. First will be those that utilize a receptionist outside the normal office or classroom configuration. In this arrangement, the receptionist is the first line of defense of the inner perimeter. The primary duties are to screen individuals that come into the facility and direct them to the location they are seeking. For those using this model, it is recommended that placement of the receptionist requires every visitor to stop and engage in conversation. The receptionist should be placed behind a barrier such as a counter to provide some reaction time should the visitor become aggressive or noncompliant. It is also recommended that the receptionist have some type of an "alert button" that will alert someone else in the immediate area when there is a situation requiring the help of another person due to the demeanor of the visitor.

Where a receptionist is not present and an inner office secretary greets visitors, it is recommended that he do so through a small window, rather than allowing the individual directly into the inner office area. This will provide the office personnel an opportunity to engage the visitor in a conversation, thus allowing them to gauge the overall demeanor. Where feasible, and if risks warrant, the use of an electronic door lock to allow entry into the inner office complex is recommended. Again, signs are important so that the expectations for visitors are clearly communicated.

Where teachers and childcare givers are tending to children, it is important that they have the ability to quickly secure office and classroom doors. Doors should be equipped with locking mechanisms that can be activated from inside the room. Interior door windows, as well as exterior wall windows, should have covers that can be used when it becomes necessary to restrict view into the room. Locations where children are housed should have a telephone, intercom, or other communication device available for the adult to use should an emergency develop and information need to be conveyed from the room. It is further recommended that adults with a view of the parking lot and walking routes of visitors be extra vigilant to watch for individuals acting suspiciously.

Visitor processing and screening

Establishing a thorough visitor processing and screening procedure is critical in an environment where children are present and given care. The procedure should be in written form, provided to the staff, and posted at locations where visitors have first contact with the inner perimeter security.

Visitor processing should begin as they arrive at the site, that is, prior to them entering the building. For facilities that provide off-street parking, it is important to identify specific and adequate parking areas for visitors. When practical, visitor parking should be in an area that can be observed by the person(s) who will ultimately be doing the screening. Where this is not possible, adults working at the facility should attempt to view visitor parking as a part of their daily routine. This provides an opportunity for staff to identify a potential threat before the person actually enters. Signs clearly identifying this area should be in place, as well as at the entry to the lot directing them where to proceed. If risk warrants, the use of closed circuit television should also be considered as a way to monitor activities in the parking lot. If closed circuit television is used, it is recommended that this fact be clearly posted on signs as persons enter the property and again at the start of the inner perimeter security. While this will not necessarily dissuade a threat from continuing, it does create a "sense of safety" for the patrons of the facility and may impact crime such as vandalism and theft.

Visitors should be required to sign a log that identifies who they are, the reason they are visiting, and the time of day. Consequently, one additional step worth considering either as a requirement, randomly, or when the "screener" is in doubt, is to require photo identification to be presented. While not every organization will want to take this step, it should be remembered that individuals on site for non-legitimate reasons might likely provide false information. More importantly, when releasing children to someone who purports to be a parent or guardian and absolute identity is not certain, it should be a requirement that photo identification be presented.

Staff assigned to screen visitors should engage them in an extended conversation. This is an excellent technique to gauge the person's demeanor, including what intentions they might have, as well as any substance they may have taken that could influence behavior.

At the location where screening takes place, it is advisable to maintain records of known domestic and child custody issues. Parents involved in child custody disputes, or where court orders have been issued, should provide copies of such. These should be readily available to the screener(s) and updated on a regular basis. It is also imperative that individual teachers be notified of child custody issues.

Visitors should wear and display a formal "visitor's badge" while on site. The badge should be dated or color-coded where staff can clearly recognize it as valid for each particular day. Badges should also be numbered and the number written in the visitor's logbook next to the individual to whom it was issued. By taking these added precautions, it will be possible to account for all visitor badges and minimize the chance and opportunity for someone to attempt to reuse a badge on another day.

Developing good visitor processing and screening procedures will work hand in hand with properly constructed access control measures. Failure to screen visitors simply negates much of the work that may have been accomplished in identifying where and how visitors access the facility. Finally, it must be remembered that screening visitors will not create an inconvenience if it is conducted in a kind, honest, and friendly manner. Due to the many acts of extreme violence occurring across the country, most patrons of the facility will appreciate all extra precautions taken.

Development and practice of crisis management plans

Crisis management plans need not be cumbersome documents. During an actual emergency, most injuries and property damage occur within the first ten minutes. Therefore, it is prudent to develop a plan for responding to those first ten minutes. The following guidelines are recommended:

- The plan should be in a format that is easily modified. Use of a three ring binder is the preferred method.
- The plan should be environmentally protected. This will ensure that when water, dirt, or debris is present, the plan is still readable. Placing pages in plastic sleeves is the preferred option.
- Information should be clearly defined and easily located through the use of a table of contents or index.
- All staff should have access to the plan and the crisis management team should have a complete copy.
- Additional copies of the plan should be placed in various locations throughout the facility, as the office may not be the most efficient or even usable place as a center of operations.
- The plan should be reviewed and updated at least once a year by more than one supervisor.

- The plan should not be wordy. The use of bulleted material is preferable to that of regular, paragraphed text because, under stress, it may be difficult to read text or locate specific information.
- Small print is hard to read under stress, so a larger font is recommended. A minimum of size 14 font is preferred and, where practical, size 16 font should be used.

The following components should be present in all crisis management plans.

Table of contents
This will allow easy referencing for each specific section being sought. It can be placed as the first page of the plan or used as the cover of the document.

Emergency management team calling tree
Each member should have a list of all the members on the team and a method to be used for calling in case of emergency. Should the need arise, this can be used to alert staff who are away from work. The calling tree can also be coded to indicate any staff members who have specialized training such as first aid, CPR, or other skills.

Team member duties and responsibilities
This should outline specific duties that may need to be performed, as well as which team member will be responsible for it. Where staffing permits, alternates should be identified. Categorically, the positions should include team leader, communications, medical, media, security, staff liaison, parent/patron liaison, plan monitor, and counseling.

Critical telephone numbers
The print in most telephone books is small and difficult to locate when under stress. Prelisting these telephone numbers can be a real time saver during an emergency event.

Sheltering and evacuation procedures

Specific procedures should be clearly written to account for fire, tornado, earthquake, hazardous material spills and leaks, as well as intruder and violent acts. How this information will be announced throughout the facility should also be included. Identified shelter areas and evacuation routes should not only be posted throughout the site, but should be written within the plan. The plan should also address how all staff and children will be accounted for and how that information will be communicated.

Event specific responses

In addition to the previous information, it is advisable to have a separate information sheet with detailed response information for a variety of specific types of emergencies such as fire, tornado, bomb threat, death, injury, or any other emergency.

Reunification site information

Specific reunification sites should be identified in the immediate vicinity. This will be important should it become necessary to quickly evacuate the building and move children to another temporary location. Ideally, the plan will have two relocation sites in opposite directions of each other, in case one site is not available. For example, where buses are available, they can become temporary housing.

Facility floor plans

The plans should identify the sheltering areas discussed earlier, as well as water-gas-electric cutoffs, location of first aid and other emergency supplies, telephones and intercoms, entrances and exits, and other facets of the facility deemed important during a time of emergency.

Critical equipment operation procedures

The plan should include information specifying how to operate critical equipment such as water-gas-electric cutoff procedures; intercoms; weather alerts or two-way radios; and other equipment.

Other sections may be necessary to include in the plan that are specific to the facility or the location. Remember, the purpose of the plan is to provide quick, easily readable information to the user during an emergency. Practicing the plan is as important as the plan itself. No one expects the event to unfold according to a script, but having practiced general scenarios will better prepare staff to respond appropriately. It is recommended that the facility's crisis management team periodically assemble and practice the plan through the use of role-playing scenarios. As the scenario creates "issues," the team needs to verify that the crisis plan addresses the needs that might arise. In using a scenario, the team should develop different options on how they might respond and then identify a series of actions that they deem appropriate.

Staff training

In addition to the traditional staff development and certifications expected of those that manage children or work in a similar environment, it is also important to incorporate non-traditional topics. Parents and patrons expect staff to be knowledgeable in first aid procedures, CPR, and basic childcare, as well as behavior management issues. However, as a society we are seeing increasingly aggressive and sometimes violent behavior from adults. Consequently, at least some of the training should focus on adult behavior management techniques.

A variety of programs are available in most communities that teach adults how to appropriately respond to escalating, aggressive, and/or violent behavior. While not intending to endorse any specific training, certain components should be present for the training to be meaningful and beneficial. Staff should be trained to recognize risk factors for both children and adults that indicate a greater chance for the behavior to manifest into aggressive actions. Although not all-inclusive, listed below are some of the more notable risk factors that should alert staff.

Outbursts of anger

Adults are generally more capable of controlling anger than children. People who exhibit displays of anger are releasing frustration in a non-productive manner and are indicating the inability to release negative feelings through other acceptable channels.

Violent acts/mental illness

Be aware of family members who have committed a violent act or who suffer from mental illness. People who have grown up in homes where violent behavior was present may believe the behavior to be more acceptable than those who did not. Some mental illnesses may be hereditary and can accentuate violent behavior.

Suicide attempts/acts of violence

Be alert for recent attempts to commit suicide and/or acts of violent behavior. Any attempt at suicide should be considered a warning sign of an emotional problem. Some of the individuals that commit violent acts are suicidal. Violent behavior is seldom an isolated event.

Coping skills

Watch for a lack of coping skills or a lack of strategies to handle personal life crises. A general lack of coping skills is prevalent in many acts of adolescent violence and may carry into adulthood. When carried into adulthood, the lack of coping skills can be more pronounced and violent.

Frequently failing to follow societal rules

Individuals who regularly fail to follow basic rules are exhibiting a tendency to disregard what most of society believes is "normal." They do not have the same perception of behavioral limits as others.

Staff training should extend beyond the recognition of escalating behavior and also include information on de-escalating and calming the individual. Time is a critical element in many acts of violence. It is important to have the skills to respond to the threat in such a manner as to either allow help to arrive, or to actually calm the person to the point that he/she can be effectively managed. Techniques such as "agreeing" with the individual can be very effective. Aggressive and/or violent people often have a grudge or feel as though they have been grieved or taken advantage of by someone. Agreeing that this may be the situation and offering sympathy, while at the same time allowing the person to talk, may gradually cause the individual to begin to de-escalate. The goal is to allow them to talk with little interruption while one is demonstrating empathy.

This type of information can only come through qualified staff development and practice. The use of role-playing, along with table-top exercises or scenarios, is an excellent method to practice appropriate responses. Trained staff will feel more secure in their abilities to respond appropriately to issues of violence and aggressive behavior and will be more likely to be effective should the day arrive when the training must be utilized.

Role of supervision

Supervision is critical and must be planned and evaluated from two perspectives. First, the presence and supervision by adults of children (and any others for which the organization has assumed responsibility) is of critical importance. Children and adolescents not only need supervision in the conventional sense, but with close adult presence they will actually feel safer. It is much the same "feeling" as seeing a law enforcement officer on patrol within a community. It is both comforting and reassuring to know that someone in authority is close at hand should a problem arise. As a result, this feeling of safety will ultimately result in greater parental confidence in the service provider as a whole. The more an adult is noticeably available to help, the more likely a child will be to confide in them when help is needed. The adult providing supervision can then notify the proper authorities if abuse, domestic issues, or issues at the site warrant further investigation.

Expectations for supervisory duties should be outlined clearly within an employee handbook. Items for inclusion within the handbook are as follows:

- Duties and responsibilities of staff
- Playground and classroom supervision expectations
- Expectations for staff conduct
- Guidelines for field trips, if applicable
- Procedures for reporting child abuse or neglect
- Child access guidelines
- Procedures for emergency drills
- Disciplinary procedures
- Process and forms for reporting accidents
- Emergency management plans
- Child privacy guidelines
- Custodial rights of parents
- Medication Procedures
- Procedures for reporting threats or other potentially dangerous situations

Employees should not only be furnished with and be required to read a handbook, but the organization should obtain a written acknowledgment from the employee that this has occurred.

Secondly, the selection process for hiring people that supervise front-line employees is of equal, if not greater, importance. When situations develop that affect the immediate safety of children and adults, it is critical that supervisors have a high tolerance for stress and proven decision-making skills. Supervisors must have a thorough understanding of organizational rules, practices, and procedures, particularly those applicable during emergency events, and they should periodically be evaluated for that knowledge. In an earlier section it was suggested that the use of tabletop exercises or role-playing through scenarios was an excellent method to test emergency management plans. This is also a good method to evaluate supervisors as to their general knowledge of organizational protocol, as well as providing a view of how one reacts while under stress. Supervisors should be expected to diligently perform all duties, as well as ensure that other employees fulfill their own duties.

Reporting and tracking system

Thorough record keeping is critically important to any organization that is a service provider or caretaker for those unable to take care of themselves, such as children and minors. Some members of society can be litigious and will hold high expectations for excellence. Consequently, facilities should implement a simple yet thorough method of processing and recording information related to safety. The following guidelines are suggested:

- A system should be in place that includes written documentation of employee notification regarding child custody orders and/or parental custody papers.
- Students and children should be signed in and out of the facility unless all arrive and are dismissed together.
- Accident reports should be written and retained for reference.
- Employees should be asked to "log" any unusual events, such as student safety concerns, custodial inquiries, or volatile employees or patrons.
- Medication forms and a record of dispensation should be retained.
- Disciplinary records should be maintained.
- Emergency parent/guardian information should be current and access controlled.
- Written record of student/child daily attendance should be kept by the teachers, as well as a copy retained within a centralized location.
- The supervisor should document the receipt of the employee handbook.

Providing safety and security for childcare and educational facilities is not as simple as making sure doors are locked. As has been illustrated in this chapter, the process is multifaceted and encompasses not only prevention strategies, but includes intervention training and response plans. While it is impossible to totally secure a facility in today's environment, patrons and parents will always seek out those that have accomplished the task to a greater degree.

Chapter 5

Responding To Medical Emergencies

Edward L. Spain, B.S.N., M.B.A., M.S. R.N. (Registered Nurse)

While singing hymns in church on Sunday morning, a panicked, "Oh my! Oh my ... help him ... someone help him!" catches your ear. From afar, you notice an elderly woman with her eyes darting along the floor and a frightened look on her face. She begins to look at the people around her and begs for someone to help. A man rises up next to her and yells, "We need help!" The singing stops quickly and people on all sides stand up to see what is happening. Others run toward the forming crowd. You hear someone yell, "I don't think he's breathing!" The helpless, hysteric cries of the frightened woman grow louder. "Does anyone know CPR?" echoes from the far side of the crowd. The churchgoer next to you whispers, "Oh, how sad."

Sadly, this scenario occurs all too often. Whether in a Sunday school classroom, a fellowship hall, a parking lot, the sanctuary, or an elevator or stairwell, church leaders have a responsibility to know what to do in a medical emergency. In a crisis situation, it is crucial to have a properly trained, knowledgeable staff that has a predetermined plan of action that will quickly and safely take care of the situation. The hesitation and hysterics that could occur due to a lack of preparation and training could cost the life of someone very dear to you.

Lifesaving measures can be accomplished through training and the development of a plan of action. The lack of training or a plan of action can prevent help from getting to the victim in a timely manner. In a medical emergency, seconds count. You are fighting the clock! Every second lost in getting to a victim and providing assistance can make the difference between a good outcome, a poor outcome, or even death.

Within this chapter we will examine the following questions: What is a medical emergency? Why is this knowledge important to you? What is a medical emergency plan and how do you develop it? What resources do you need? Who can help you? What equipment do you need to purchase? It's an emergency — what do you do?

What Is A Medical Emergency?

A medical emergency is anything that affects a person's **A**irway, **B**reathing, or **C**irculation (ABCs) and is beyond your ability to fix. In short, medical help is needed. Let us first begin by defining these terms more precisely. The first term, "airway," is the tube that allows air to pass from the mouth into the lungs. It can become blocked by an obstruction or by damage to the nose or mouth. It may also be blocked by fluids such as water or blood. "Breathing" is the act of taking air into the lungs by expanding the chest. Sometimes the drive that causes the body to take a breath is not present or is temporarily altered. Air must get to the lungs so the blood can pick up the oxygen in the air and deliver it to individual cells throughout the body. This act of transportation by the blood is called "circulation." All three components must be present at all times for the human body to function properly.

Pertaining to these three bodily functions/parts, the most common problems are stroke, cardiac arrest or arrhythmia, shock, obstructed airway, or choking. The bottom line is, if someone is in distress for any reason, get medical help on the way as soon as possible. This is an integral part of providing CPR or first aid.

Why Is This Important?

Suppose your pastor or a staff member is walking to the pulpit and suddenly collapses. What would happen? Would he or she survive? Someone's grandchild is playing with her friends in her toddler Sunday school class when she reaches down and picks up a button that has fallen off another child's coat. She immediately puts the button in her mouth and within twenty seconds is turning blue and is unable to make a sound. What will that Sunday school teacher do? In either of the situations just mentioned, the actions taken in the next 1-2 minutes will greatly affect not only the lives of the victims, but also the lives of everyone in their family and church family.

Why is this important? First, you must accept the fact that such emergencies are not a matter of *if* they will occur; it is a matter of *when* they will occur. Since the human body is not perfect and does not last forever, it is most certainly susceptible to failure somewhere along the way. Ask yourself, "Am I prepared to do what it will take to help someone survive a medical emergency?" If you are prepared, this is not a frightening concept. In fact, there are a few simple things you can learn that will give any victim the best possible chance of recovery. Fear comes from knowing you are not prepared to handle a medical emergency. Sadly enough, we often assume that it will happen, yet remain unprepared. Statistics say it will happen. Mothers, fathers, grandparents, pastors, children, greeters, Sunday school teachers, and all the rest of us make up those statistics.

As we discussed earlier, the most common problems are stroke, cardiac arrest or rhythm problems, shock, obstructed airway, or choking. Understanding a little about these processes can help you recognize their threats. By recognizing these risks, you will remain in control of the situation rather than allowing panic and a sense of helplessness to direct your actions.

We will look at the facts concerning each process. What are the symptoms? (That is, what you should look for?) What should you do? What should you avoid? Remember, this chapter is not designed to create a medical professional. Rather, it is designed to give you a rudimentary knowledge of the subject, which in a crisis situation can help save someone's life.

According to the American Heart Association, this year approximately 2 million people in the United States will be diagnosed with an Acute Coronary Syndrome (ACS). The Department of Health and Human Services reports more than one-half million people will be hospitalized with a diagnosis of unstable angina (chest pain at rest or with exertion) and one-and-a-half million will experience an Acute Myocardial Infarction (AMI) or heart attack. Of these, approximately fifty percent will be sudden and one-half million will die, according to the *Journal of American College of Cardiology*. The early warning signs of a cardiac event include:

- Indigestion
- Shortness of breath
- Discomfort in the center of the chest. Discomfort may extend into one or both arms, the neck, jaws, upper abdomen, or even into the back

Some people experience pain or discomfort in some of these areas alone without involving the chest. Do not ignore chest pain! The American Heart Association describes the sensation as " pain, pressure, fullness, squeezing, aching, heaviness, tightness, burning, or numbness." Heart attack victims frequently deny the possibility they are having a heart attack. They often begin looking for reasons why that can't happen. This type of behavior should be considered a warning sign, and you should take immediate action. If you get the person to the hospital in time, it may be possible to open a blocked vessel to restore circulation and prevent permanent damage to the heart muscle.

Stroke is the third leading cause of death in the United States and the leading cause of brain death in adults. The American Stroke Association reports in the United States approximately 500,000 persons suffer a stroke each year, and nearly a quarter of these victims die. The warning signs of a stroke (brain attack) include:

- Dimness or loss of vision
- Sudden severe headache
- Unexplained dizziness or falls
- Weakness or numbness on one side of the body
- Difficulty talking or understanding speech

If you notice any of these sudden changes, seek medical attention immediately. The *New England Journal of Medicine* introduced therapies that should be considered for all patients taken to the hospital within three hours of the onset of signs and symptoms consistent with an acute stroke. These therapies may or may not be available in your local hospital but emergency services personnel will know the closest facility available.

Stroke victims must be dealt with quickly. Every second that brain tissue goes without a blood supply, the cells in the brain are deprived of oxygen that is needed for it to function properly. Consequently, the risk of death increases. As time passes, these cells may actually die. If the blood supply is not restored quickly, all the cells dependent on that vessel for oxygen will die along with their specific function. Those cells along the "motor strip" that allow you to move your arms and legs can be affected and die if the vessel that supplies blood to them gets clogged. The longer the vessel is clogged or blood is not flowing, the more tissue will die.

According to *Emergency Medicine Clinics of North America*, electrical shock is responsible for 5,000 victims annually requiring emergency treatment and for 500 to 1,000 deaths. Electrical shock victims can experience a wide variety of injuries, both internal as well as external. If you touch a victim of electrical shock you could receive an electric shock yourself. Their muscles will contract because of the electrical current passing through them. They will be unable to speak or let go. Most importantly, do not put yourself at risk. Do not enter the proximity of live current; this requires specially trained personnel. You should immediately turn off the power and call for help.

Choking and obstructed airway can result from a foreign object, regurgitation or bleeding, even an unresponsive victim's tongue. Choking results in over 3,000 deaths annually according to the National Safety Council. Choking in adults usually occurs during eating. Small children are at high risk. Choking should be suspected when a person:

- suddenly develops difficulty breathing.

- becomes cyanotic (slightly bluish, grayish, slatelike, or dark purple discoloration of the skin).
- becomes unconscious for no apparent reason.

Furthermore, everyone should be made aware that the universal sign of a choking victim is both hands grasping the throat and an inability to speak.

What Does Our Church Need To Purchase?

The key pieces of medical equipment are an Automated External Defibrillator (AED) discussed later in the chapter, a pocket mask, and a first aid kit. The pocket mask is a valuable piece of equipment. This device prevents direct contact with oral secretions and allows for the ventilation of the victim. Often, people won't tell you, or are unable to tell you, if they have diseases because of the social stigma associated with it. This can provide hesitation on the part of potential rescuers that can cost a victim his life. A rescuer does not want to provide the service and then find out a serious or potentially life-threatening disease has been contracted from the victim. Pocket masks come in a variety of styles and costs. Talk with your local emergency services personnel to see which style they recommend. You can often purchase masks through your local hospital, emergency medical or ambulance service, fire department, or police department.

First aid kits can be made up from supplies obtained at your local store. There are some basics that can be placed in a tackle box marked with a large red cross. These include a roll bandage, 4x4 gauze, scissors, tape, adhesive bandages (various sizes), triple antibiotic ointment, triangle bandage or sling, ibuprofen, aspirin, chemical cold packs, and an inventory list. Small plastic locking tags will let you know if someone has used something out of the kit and will remind you to restock it. Sizes of kits will vary and should be determined by the number of incidents you are treating and the type of situations most common in your area.

After purchasing the items needed for the kit, remember to make the best of your investment by following simple rules: replace used items and check expiration dates. Using a checklist is important, for it is a common problem that someone uses an item and no one knows it until the next time there is an emergency, which can prove disastrous. Some of the items in the first aid kits could have expiration dates, and they should be checked carefully. If no expiration date is on the package or if it has somehow been obscured, you should replace it.

Basic first aid classes can be obtained from most local emergency medical services (ambulance and fire) personnel and the Red Cross. Many will volunteer their time to train your staff.

Medical emergency resources should be discussed with the congregation of the church to heighten awareness and preparedness. Keep a log of CPR instructors and class locations, resources, and resource people to help others get prepared. Volume purchasing of masks, AEDs, and first aid supplies can help make preparation more affordable for smaller churches.

Checklists of supplies need to be completed on a regular basis by a staff member or a maintenance team. Checklists assure that the equipment which is required in your medical emergency plan is in its assigned location and is in good working order. If first aid kits have been used, make sure the supplies are replenished.

What Is A Medical Emergency Plan?

The goal of a medical emergency plan is to get help to the person in need of medical attention as quickly as possible.

There are four links in the American Heart Association "Chain of Survival":

1. Early access to Emergency Medical Services (EMS)
2. Early CPR
3. Early defibrillation (stopping the quivering or ineffective contractions of the heart through drugs or an electrical device)
4. Early advanced cardiovascular care

If any one of these links is weak or missing, the survival rate decreases. These are addressed below.

A significant issue to be addressed by church leadership is who is responsible for what. The purpose of this section is to address this issue. To begin, someone must call for help. This may include an ambulance, fire department, or the local police department. All local emergency services telephone numbers need to be quickly available to anyone in the church. Having a list of all emergency response numbers clearly posted on or near telephones is ideal. Sometimes emergency medical providers, such as ambulance, fire department, and police department, will provide a sticker bearing their telephone number that can be placed on all telephones throughout the church. This is greatly simplified if your area has a 911 system. The 911 system is designed to simplify contacting emergency assistance providers and deliver a faster response by emergency assistance. An enhanced 911 option automatically provides communications operators with the caller's address and telephone number. If your community does not have a 911 service, take steps to get it in your community. Contact your local emergency services and local government officials.

In the stressful situation of a medical emergency, you will find looking up even simple telephone numbers very difficult and time consuming. Once the call is made, the caller must stay on the telephone with the communications operator to provide critical information to EMS responders about the type of emergency, the location, and other information.

The second step in the "Chain of Survival" is to provide CPR. Training people in CPR and the use of AEDs has saved countless lives that might otherwise have been lost. CPR training is offered through your local or regional American Heart Association or Red Cross office at little or no cost. In addition, your local hospital, ambulance service, police, or fire departments will also be able to provide this information. This training will include management of an obstructed airway (choking victim). The Heimlich maneuver is used to create an artificial cough and is part of the CPR class content.

Someone on the paid church staff, as well as several volunteer workers, must be CPR and first aid certified. The number of people required that should receive this training may depend on the size of your church and the number of worship services offered. It is important to have enough people trained and certified to provide adequate coverage when services are in session and during staff office hours throughout the week. Larger churches with multiple staff members should encourage CPR training for their entire staff, including Sunday school teachers and children's ministry workers.

CPR is certification for a period of time and does require re-certification when it expires. Your CPR and first aid training provider will tell you how long your certification lasts before recertification is required. Being aware of this will enable you to recertify before your certification expires. It is also a good idea to have some people in your congregation trained as CPR trainers, which will facilitate recertification of your staff.

According to the *Annals of Emergency Medicine* and *New England Journal of Medicine*, early defibrillation is the link in the survival chain that is most likely to improve survival rates. The key to survival from an out-of-hospital cardiac arrest is through placing AEDs in the hands of large numbers of trained rescuers. Survival rates of 89 percent have been reported with early CPR and early defibrillation. Every minute that passes between collapse and defibrillation reduces the chance of successful conversion by seven to ten percent. The goal is to return spontaneous circulation, which increases survival and decreases long-term complications.

AEDs are extremely simple to operate and the required training is minimal. This is a small portable device, about the size of a small tackle box, which is designed to deliver an electrical charge through patches placed on the victim's chest. This electrical charge will allow the heart's normal pacemaker to take over. The AED provides instructions that assist with the operation of the device that virtually eliminates mistakes. There is no reason to be afraid of an AED unit. The training removes any anxiety and fear that can result in hesitation. It will save lives. AED training is available through the CPR course providers in your area.

To permit and encourage AED use in the public, nearly all states have developed supportive legislation. The Cardiac Arrest Survival Act provides immunity for lay rescuers and businesses that use and/or purchase AEDs for public access defibrillation. Many states have specifically added provisions to their Good Samaritan Laws. You must have formal training in CPR and the use of an AED by a nationally recognized course. The American Heart Association provides education geared toward lay people. Remember — "Don't wait to defibrillate."

Medical Emergency Response Team

Second Baptist Church in Springfield, Missouri, has an excellent protocol for the medical emergency response team they have called "Second Responders." According to the program's creator, Debbie Ream, R.N., Second Responders is made up of members of Second Baptist Church who receive specific training to provide medical care to anyone in need while attending church services. Various members of Second Responders are assigned to be on-call at specific worship services. During their assigned service, the team members carry a pager that can be called by any member of the congregation whenever a medical emergency occurs. The pager number is listed in various church publications and on small cards that are available throughout the church.

Second Responders have access to an AED and a first aid kit to treat any medical emergency that occurs. The team members must be CPR and AED certified and possess basic medical knowledge. The members of Second Responders are made up of doctors, nurses, nurse practitioners, physical therapists, dieticians, and others in medical related occupations.

How Second Responders operates
- When a page is received by a team member of Second Responders notifying him or her of a medical emergency, the team member is to proceed to the nearest AED. They

are to always take the AED with them regardless of the nature of the medical emergency reported.

- Respond to the location reported via the pager. If the pager information does not indicate the location of the medical emergency, the team member is to wait at the office for someone to come to them.
- Upon arrival at the location of the medical emergency, quickly assess the emergency. For example, determine if the patient is breathing, has a pulse, or is unresponsive.
- Call 911 as soon as possible. If in doubt that emergency medical personnel are required, always err on the side of safety. It is the team members' responsibility to call 911 or to direct someone else to do so. Be sure the caller directs emergency medical personnel to the entrance of the church that is closest to the patient. It is also a good idea to have someone meet the paramedics or fire department personnel in order to ensure their arrival as soon as possible.
- Perform a complete assessment of the patient and prepare to use the AED, the first aid kit, or to perform CPR, whichever is the appropriate treatment.
- After the rescue, the team member will document in writing what occurred recording pertinent information about the patient and what was done.

The protocol of Second Responders also provides detailed information as to how to operate the AED.

It is important that churches contact their local hospital or fire department in order to become aware of the policies and regulations involved in providing this service to your congregation. For example, because an AED device is considered medical equipment, in some areas of the country you may need to secure a physician's prescription in order to purchase and use an AED.

How Do I Develop A Medical Emergency Plan And Who Can Help?

The key to a successful response to medical emergencies is organization and planning. It is suggested to develop a list of all medical professionals in your church and include them in your medical emergency plan. It is important that the staff is aware of the identity of these individuals. Creating a photo list to assist in identifying these individuals may prove helpful. Contacting your local hospital, ambulance, fire or police departments will also provide excellent resource people. The level of emergency medical care varies tremendously across the United States and from region to region. It is important that you follow the guidance of your local emergency medical care providers. The information contained in this chapter will assist the emergency medical providers in your area to work with you in developing a plan for your church. They may have questions or additional recommendations specific to their jurisdiction. Another reason for sharing your medical emergency plan with the local medical emergency providers is to develop a relationship with them and to maximize the resources that are available. Your local medical emergency providers are pleased to assist you in developing your medical emergency plan before an incident occurs.

Prior to the occurrence of a medical emergency, designate people to carry out five tasks. They are:

1. Command
2. Stay with the victim
3. Call for help
4. Obtain medical equipment (AED, pocket mask, first aid kit, if indicated)
5. Create crowd control and access to the victim

The individuals who carry out these tasks should be those most likely to be present. This may include paid staff. It may be necessary for larger churches to designate groups of individuals for different buildings or sections (sanctuary, adult, children, seniors, and youth). Train managerial staff members, leaders, and teachers to take on this role if assigned individuals are not present. Your medical emergency plan should not be a secret. Annual or semiannual education is necessary to assure that everyone understands their roles. Your medical emergency plan will show the congregation and the public that you care about them and their families.

Now let's examine the five tasks.

1. Who will be in charge in case of an emergency? The command person must immediately recognize your pre-assigned individuals, and if those individuals are not immediately present, to assign the following responsibilities. This is the individual who, according to your medical emergency plan, is in charge of the incident and ensures that each facet of the plan is being carried out. Take charge of the situation! This individual will provide a sense of security and provide direction to organize efforts to get help. It is important to know who has been trained for a crisis situation and who will be responsible for putting your training into action. This will eliminate lost time and confusion that always occur during a high-stress crisis situation.

2. Assign someone to stay with the victim. This individual optimally should know CPR and/or basic first aid. This individual's role is to provide a sense of security to the victim and assist by supporting the ABCs if needed. Is the victim breathing (actually moving air into his or her lungs) and is there a pulse? If they have been trained to provide CPR, they should begin to do so. If they have not been trained, they must rely on the arrival of emergency medical personnel.

3. Who will call for help? When the incident occurs, someone must be assigned to call for emergency services. This will get rescue personnel moving toward you as soon as possible. It is important to stay on the telephone with the communications operator and respond to all questions. The

communications operator may require directions or ask you to look for and signal emergency personnel to assist in locating the quickest way to get to the victim. Have someone go to the church parking lot to more quickly direct them to the victim. Emergency beacons may be especially beneficial for rural areas in order for rescuers to quickly locate the victim at night. Assure that the street numbers on your church are easily visible. They should be large and clearly visible from the road. Check with your local fire district and city regulations.

4. Who will obtain medical equipment? Your plan must include the manner in which a person is designated to get the equipment required for the medical emergency. The location of medical equipment (AED, first aid kit, CPR mask) must be visible and clearly marked. Place it in a cabinet on the wall or on a shelf. You might even want to mark the area with a large red cross. The equipment should be checked and inspected regularly according to the manufacturer's recommendation. Place the equipment on a maintenance checklist so it is not missed. There is nothing more frustrating than a piece of neglected medical equipment that fails to operate because routine maintenance was not provided or the battery was not changed.

5. As part of the medical emergency plan, there should be those who are charged with the responsibility of crowd control. This person must clear the immediate area and make a path for emergency personnel to get to the victim. Crowds of people or obstacles can delay rescuers and result in unnecessary harm to the victim.

Even though these tasks are addressed separately, each of them should be performed simultaneously. Remember, planning for a medical emergency will provide the best possible chance for a good outcome.

It's A Medical Emergency, What Do I Do?

Is your church prepared for a medical emergency? If a member of the staff or congregation were to experience a cardiac arrest would they survive? If you are unsure or the answer is "No," now is the time to take action. Plan for the protection of everyone in your church. Follow the simple steps outlined in the chapter. There is a medical emergency plan outline at the end of this chapter. Too often, following a crisis, people say, "We talked about what we needed to do, we just never did it. Now it's too late." Give them every possible advantage to not only survive but to return to the fullness of their life, without complications. Your church can be prepared for medical emergencies! Begin today, tomorrow may be too late!

Medical Emergency Plan Outline

(Your Church) Medical Emergency Plan

Trained medical personnel in our church: _____

_____

_____

CPR-certified staff: _____

_____

_____

Designate people to five tasks: (large churches designate teams per area)
1. Command _____
2. Stay with the victim _____
3. Call for help (911) _____
4. Emergency numbers (assure phone number stickers are at every phone)
   Emergency medical services or
   Ambulance service _____
   Police department _____
   Fire department _____
5. Obtaining medical equipment (AED, pocket mask, emergency beacon, first aid kit, if indicated)

Location of equipment _____

Designated individual(s) _____

Equipment check schedule _____

Crowd control and access to the victim _____

Date for next Emergency Medical Plan education and review

_____

Chapter 6

Establishing A Church Security Officer Program

John M. Edie, B.A., M.R.E.

He greeted everyone he met at church that day with a gracious smile and a friendly "Hello." He made his way through the Sunday school meeting areas, the worship center and into closets and darkened hallways. Ultimately, he walked into the preschool section and talked to the children and even picked up a toddler and gave a loving hug. Within seconds an alert preschool caregiver became highly suspicious and called the church security department, which alerted the church staff member in charge of security.

The above scenario was an actual occurrence. It could have been a crisis situation, but it has a positive ending. The gentleman was an out-of-town friend of the author. As a method to evaluate security issues in the church, I asked him to have free roam of the building and see what he could do and where he could go. A luncheon had been previously scheduled for church leadership to take place after the morning worship service to discuss issues pertaining to safety and security. At that luncheon, my friend was introduced and the leadership staff was told of his activities during the few preceding hours. The group was astounded at the *stranger's* ease of access as he was allowed into supposedly secure areas. Needless to say, a few changes occurred during the next week involving the church's security plan.

Having a workable security plan and security officer organization has become more and more of a necessity of life for North American churches. Though the structural differences vary from urban to rural settings, it remains a fact that no church facilities or congregations are wholly immune to violence, disruption, emergencies, or theft.

Churches and their leadership must understand they have a responsibility to be pro-active and reactive in the protection and well-being of their members and adherents. This varies from designating safe places for purses of ladies in the church choir to the observance of parking lots. The issue is not whether to have a security plan or mindset, but what the security plan will entail.

Discerning The Need

In recent years there have been many incidents of inappropriate and illegal behavior displayed in our nation's churches. This consists of violence, sexual misconduct, and theft, just to name a few. For example, Richard Dearsmith, a man with an extensive criminal record, entered a church in Colorado Springs, Colorado. As the ushers were taking the offering through the foyer to be counted, Dearsmith attempted to wrestle away an offering plate from one of the ushers. The usher grabbed the offering plate back and Dearsmith ran out of the church. Consequently, a member of the congregation called the police. As the police were searching for Dearsmith, he returned to the church and began verbally harassing the ushers who were standing at the rear of the church. He then walked into a restroom at which time a quick thinking church worker locked the door to the restroom and notified the police, who minutes later entered the restroom where Dearsmith brandished a knife with a seven-inch blade. The situation became so hostile that a police officer was forced to shoot him. Unfortunately, Dearsmith died as a result of the gunshot wound.

In this example, two individuals were instrumental in successfully dealing with this hostile situation: the member of the congregation who first called the police and the church worker who locked Dearsmith in the bathroom. Although this situation ended tragically, the consequences could have been much worse for members of the congregation. It is therefore the burden of churches to prepare individuals to act in situations that may require quick, decisive action. It is the intent of this chapter to assist churches in developing a security officer team who will have the ability to deal with these types of situations and much more.

Though most church leaders know from experience that there is a need, they usually have little, if any, formal training in leading or developing a functional security plan. Therefore, the first issue that must be addressed is the need for an organized security officer program.

Organization And Leadership

Generally, the most effective way to approach the development of a workable security officer program is for members of the congregation with some affinity or experience in security techniques or law enforcement to lead in the process.

In conjunction with these individuals, the direction and coordination of the security officer program should rest with a specified full-time church staff member or a security committee. In an appropriate setting, the staff member or committee members should explain to the congregation the need to address security and safety issues and how they intend to accomplish it. In so doing, the security officer program will enjoy the support and encouragement of the congregation. The formation of a church security officer program should be formally approved by the church and consequently the congregation should be notified when the program begins.

Under the coordination and leadership of the full-time staff member, the security team leader should have someone in direct supervision of the team members on duty. Normally, it is best if the security leader works under the church administrator or Christian education director who serves as the program's coordinator. In smaller churches, this person may be accountable to the pastor. This gives accountability to the full-time staff and positions him to have availability for input into needs or changes. As a recognized church leader, the security team leader is to be held to the same expectations as staff, deacons, and Sunday school leadership.

The security team should be divided into sub-groups that function during assigned services. Sub-group captains should be given leadership responsibility for their group's duties at the assigned time. It is important to alternate teams to afford every security team member the opportunity to attend worship services and other church-sponsored activities.

Of paramount importance is the understanding of the role those involved in the security officer program will play. The security team is not a legally empowered police force. Team members are not to see their function as secret service agents or undercover police officers watching every move made by each individual entering the church facility. They should not even be called a security staff or officers. It is best to refer to them as the security committee or team. These individuals are servants fulfilling service responsibilities for the congregation.

It is also important that the security leader be in full agreement with the policies and direction of the church. This is critically important when having to deal with situations that may have negative overtones or implications. He is to be a model of godly leadership as well as godly followship. A cooperative team spirit from the leader will set the tone for the team members. There should never be any question but that the security team is 100 percent involved and supportive of all of what the church is about. This begins with the example of the security team leader.

Not that there are any unimportant positions of ministry in the local church, but the security team must include individuals who can be trusted with the safety of the congregation. The following qualifications or characteristics are recommended for the leader and members of the security team. Each of these people must:

- be a committed Christian who has consistently demonstrated a life of service to God.
- be an active member in good standing and integrally involved in the church's ministry. This includes regular worship service attendance and active involvement in small group (Sunday school) and other ministry activities of the church.
- be a person who is known by and highly respected by the congregation.

- demonstrate a lifestyle that is consistent with what God and the church expects of its leaders.
- be a person that reflects honesty, integrity, compassion, and fairness.
- be a person of obvious maturity.
- be faithful in tithing and financial support of the church.
- be free of any criminal history.

It is critical that the members of the church security organization understand their service role and gel as a positive functioning team. Being a model of positive involvement in the life of the church gives great credibility to the actions taken by the security team. Just as the pastor and staff are to lead holy lives, so, too, are all of the ministry positions in the church, including security team members. They are first and foremost models of persons who have a deep, personal relationship with Jesus Christ.

Chain Of Command Of Security Organization
Coordinator
(Senior pastor/executive pastor/associate pastor)
Security Team Leader
(Volunteer worker/church staff member)
Sub-group Captains
(Volunteer workers)
Team Members
(Volunteer workers)

Recruitment Of Team Members

Now that we have discussed the qualifications of the security team leader and members, it is a good time to discuss the selection process. Because of the nature of the position, it is recommended that the full-time church staff member and the volunteer leader of the security team actively recruit people who they believe possess the qualifications previously addressed. Therefore, it is not recommended to merely accept applications or allow people to volunteer in order to avoid hurting people's feelings. Whatever recruitment process is implemented by your church, it will be necessary to have some method of gently weeding out those individuals who do not meet the qualifications.

Recruiting for the security team must be done in compliance with the desires of church leadership. It is imperative that the security team members reflect the highest standards of godly behavior. The issue of safety and orderly conduct are to be handled and demonstrated from a heart of love and kindness. Regardless of the severity of a situation, the heart of Jesus must be demonstrated. It must never be forgotten that someone from the unchurched world is watching every move the church makes. Our image needs to reflect the highest level of compassion and integrity.

Although it may be beneficial in some ways, being a former or current law enforcement officer is not enough to qualify a person for a position on the church security officer program. The position is as much godliness driven as it is experience driven. Much of the success of any church security officer program will be predicated in large part on the image and trustworthiness of the leader.

Operation Of The Security Program

The operation of the security team should consist of two interrelated strategies, visible (overt) presence and invisible (covert) presence. A visible presence could be accomplished through regular walking patterns in each part of the facility and parking lots. Being visible and serving as roving goodwill ambassadors is very important. A smile, kind word, helping guests with directions, and assisting those with physical disabilities are a shining example of the security team. They become servants instead of wardens. It is always incumbent on the security team to remember that the mission of the church is to be an example of Christ.

The look and demeanor of the security team should be indicative of the openness and wholeness of the church body as a whole. Security team members should wear appropriate nametags that identify them as security personnel. There are many other ways that security team members can be recognized by the congregation such as shirts or blazers on which "Security" or "Security Team" can be embroidered. Regardless of the manner that security team members are identified, the presentation should be pleasant, nonthreatening, and welcoming to the congregation. The first person a member or guest should seek out for direction, general information, or emergency assistance is a member of the security team.

Members of the security team should display conduct that is mature and confident. The display of godliness in crisis situations greatly increases the chances of a calm resolution and positive outcome. The purpose of the security officer team is to put people at ease and project a belief that "all is well." This atmosphere of assurance is best accomplished by persons of strong spiritual stature and good reputation.

The responsibilities of the security team may vary greatly depending on the needs of your church. Responsibilities may include, but are not limited to the following:

- Visual monitoring of the nursery areas, small group (Sunday school) classrooms, and worship services
- Dealing with emergency situations
- Parking lot surveillance
- Platform security
- Being present while the offering is counted
- Being dispensers of information, such as the location of Sunday school rooms, restrooms, sanctuary, and other areas

Additionally, there should be predetermined guidelines regarding how the security team is to respond in a particular situation. For example, if an elderly person falls in the building or in the parking lot, or if someone experiences a cardiac arrest, what should they do? Several issues must be addressed. This will include:

- Who will respond
- What will be done and by whom

- If the situation warrants, who is responsible for calling emergency personnel
- When should a service be disrupted to get needed assistance

If the church has an emergency response plan, every security team member should be well versed in evacuation and safety procedures. Whatever the situation, the team member should have advanced instruction in what to do. (See ch. 5 for a response plan for emergency situations.)

Specific target areas should be known to every security team member. For example, children's areas are to be constantly monitored. Security team members should always know who is in charge in the children's area and understand the expectations of the children's ministry staff. The security team needs to be alerted to any concern a parent may express related to a family member who may be unauthorized to pick up a child. Instances such as these require loving but firm handling and are a possibility for police intervention.

Other instances when police should be summoned are:

- A child's safety is being threatened by an adult
- Spouse conflict that presents a dangerous situation for their children and others
- Persons who become belligerent or display assaultive behavior and refuse to leave
- Any immediate threat to the safety and well-being of those in attendance

Church offerings present another opportunity for involvement of the security team. Depending on how the offering is handled in your church, you may wish to have a security team member present while the offering is being counted and processed by the ushers. You may also desire that security team members make the deposit at the bank. Visible presence of the security team related to money issues can be very important since questionable situations or appearances can lead to eroding of confidence or spreading of rumor about financial impropriety.

Finally, it must be remembered that every security team member should understand they are not to put themselves in a situation that can easily lead to bodily harm. Every effort should be made to resolve situations with godliness and common sense and not by brute force. There are times when force is needed, but it should be as a last resort. Generally, uniformed police officers or security guards providing uniformed security throughout the church campus is unnecessary and ill advised. However, if the church receives specific threats or other information that would indicate an imminent threat or harm, church leadership may want to consider uniformed, armed, off-duty police officers or security personnel.

Having completed our discussion of the visible, or overt, presence that the security team should display in church, it now remains to discuss invisible, or covert, presence. Although this is somewhat difficult to acknowledge, there may be a need for invisible or covert presence of security team members. There are many documented occasions when the senior pastor or a member of the pastoral staff has received credible threats to their safety, for many pastors are well known and highly visible in their communities as well as on a national level. This has been known to attract people who suffer from mental illness or merely display behavior that may be perceived as a threat to physical safety. Given this, it is recommended that a member of the security team be assigned to the worship center during each service. This person should be seated near the front of the worship center in relatively close proximity to the platform, but in a position to avoid being noticed by the congregation. The recommended place for the team member is to the side with a clear view of the platform and the closest entrance and exit doors near the front of the worship center.

The primary role of this team member is to provide protection for those on the platform and intervene in the event when it would be obvious that an approach to the platform is inappropriate and unnecessary. He will help to restore order in any form of service disruption and assist in dealing with an emergency situation. The author recommends that the team member receive direction from, or "key off" of the pastoral staff member who serves as the coordinator of the security program. For example, if there is a disruption in the sanctuary or if for any reason the coordinator leaves the sanctuary, the security team member assigned to the sanctuary is to follow. This provides an invaluable comfort level to the church staff to know assistance will be almost instantaneous.

Church staff and security team members should also know if police professionals are in attendance in the worship service. If a threatening situation is possible, the police officer should be alerted in advance in case help is needed.

There may be occasions when it is necessary for a member of the security team to approach the worship leader or pastor while at the pulpit during a service. Security team members should know when and how to approach the worship leader or pastor during a worship service regarding emergency situations. In order to avoid confusion, as well as unnecessarily disrupting the service and disturbing the congregation, there should be clearly defined guidelines regarding, who, what, and when this is to be done. For example, a locked car with its headlights on is not an emergency situation. A person experiencing a cardiac arrest in the worship center is an emergency. Security personnel must have an understanding of what constitutes an emergency. Each church will need to construct their own definition of "emergency situation" and then develop their policy accordingly.

One of the decisions church leadership will have to consider is the number of security team members that is required to give the appropriate amount of security coverage. Even though there is no specific formula to use, the considerations in order to answer this question are the number of people attending church services and other meetings, and the size and layout of the church facility and campus. Also, the number of entrances to the church may play a role in determining how many security team members are needed. The church facility should be divided into segments and the appropriate number of security team members be assigned to each segment. Key hallway intersections and children's areas should always be monitored.

If the church utilizes surveillance/security cameras, a member of the security team should be assigned to carefully observe the monitors during service times. This gives much wider possibility for action during times of need and can supplement the security team's efforts. (See ch. 7 for information regarding security/surveillance cameras.)

There is, finally, one more consideration. The work of the security team is not to be the subject of open conversation. Difficult or embarrassing situations involving members or guests should be kept within the confines of the security team and church staff. Discretion, integrity, and confidentiality are to be trademarks of each security team member.

Use Of Equipment

Churches may want to consider the use of equipment that can facilitate their mission of providing security measures to the congregation. One of the best tools a church can provide for the security team is some form of wireless communication. For any agile, responsive, security team, two-way radios are a necessity. Being able to stay in contact with other team members is very important. There are a variety of inexpensive two-way radios currently on the market. They give instant access between team members and greatly enhance the speed for dealing with crisis situations. With the advent of wireless telephones that have two-way radio features, teams can be at instant disposal, in addition to having the capability of an emergency telephone. At least one member of the security team on duty must have a cellular telephone on his person.

Many churches use golf carts as visible images in monitoring the church parking lots. The golf cart should be clearly labeled and be a welcome sight to those needing assistance or a dreaded sight to those intent on mischief. The golf cart can also be used as a shuttle to those having difficulty in walking long distances. These vehicles not only facilitate the mission of security but also enhance the service aspect of the security team.

In contemporary society, we have many examples of violent acts enacted against church leaders and congregants that have

111

resulted in tragic loss of life and serious physical injury, theft, or other adverse consequences. Because we cannot pretend that these incidents do not occur, consideration must be given in the event these situations occur. Church leadership will also have to struggle with the dilemma of whether or not to utilize law enforcement related tools and weapons such as firearms, pepper spray, hand-cuffs, or devices used to physically control people who pose an imminent threat to the safety of the congregation. Generally speaking, the use of such weapons or devices is not advised and may be deemed inappropriate in a church setting. However, depending on the security needs of the church, these tools are available as long as the security team members are trained in their use and implementation. It is the author's opinion that weapons and other law enforcement tools should not be utilized by church security team members. If a situation occurs that may require such action, this is likely an opportunity to involve law enforcement in dealing with those situations. Churches also need to be aware of the legal liability attached to using weapons and other devices or tools.

If there is a credible security threat present, which indicates that weapons and other law enforcement related tools might be necessary, this would extend beyond the purpose and expertise of the security team. If church leadership believes their level of security should be at that level, a professional security company or off-duty police officer should be employed.

Sample Church Security Guidelines

Whatever you determine will be the purpose and mission of your security team, general responsibilities should be provided to the team members in written form. A security team without clear focus will prove to be gravely deficient when called upon to respond.

In order to assist church leaders in establishing a church security officer program, sample "Security Officer Program Guidelines" are included below that can be tailored to accommodate any church.

(Sample)
Community Church
State, City
Security Officer Program Guidelines

One of the first people a member or guest often sees when arriving at the Community Church campus is a member of the church security officer team. How a person is treated on their first contact will in large part determine that person's total experience for their visit to our church. Security team members must always remember we never get a second chance to make a good first impression. In fact, if we don't make a good first impression, we may never get the opportunity to make another impression of any kind.

People come with all kinds of cares, hurts, disappointments, sorrows, and needs. What we must remember is that it is not their attitude toward us that really matters, but our attitude in response to them that counts. We must radiate with every part of our being that every guest and member has entered a place of healing, comfort, joy, positive attitudes, stability, and order.

Expectations of security team members

1. Have a personal, intimate, relationship with Jesus Christ demonstrated by a life of service to God
2. Be an active member in good standing. This includes regular attendance in the church's worship service and other church activities
3. Must demonstrate a lifestyle that is consistent with what God and the church expects of its leaders
4. Be a person that reflects honesty, integrity, compassion, and fairness
5. Be a person of obvious maturity
6. Must have a clean criminal history
7. Faithful in tithing and financial support of the church
8. Exhibit a servant's image
9. Faithful in being at assigned place
10. Know security officer program team responsibilities and procedures

Procedural guidelines

1. Remember you represent Jesus Christ, regardless of the situation.
2. Never forget there is not a time when you will need to be rude, hateful, or ungodly in your actions. The image, regardless of how firm it may have to be, is always positive and respectful in nature.
3. Greet everyone you meet. Let them see and hear a person who radiates the joy that Jesus gives.
4. Do not unduly place yourself in a dangerous situation. The police should be called immediately in cases such as a person with a gun or knife or a hostage situation.
5. Be alert to any unusual activity in parking lots and in the building. Report any disturbance to the security officer program team leader. The police department should only be contacted by the security officer program team leader or his designee.
6. Every disturbance or accident on the property needs to be immediately reported to the security officer program team leader and documented in written form. Forms are available from the security team cabinets in the church office. Completed forms should be sealed in the envelope provided and placed in the designated receptacle in the cabinet.
7. Be available to provide any assistance needed in time of physical emergency.
8. Be familiar with the first aid equipment and its use. Periodic training in CPR and use of the church AED equipment will be offered.

Conclusion

Again, it is unfortunate that we have to address the need for safety and security measures within the local church, but it has become a sad fact of life. The church in North America has not been spared the bloodshed and violence that have become commonplace in other parts of the world. We know that until Jesus returns, the church will be the prime target of Satan and we should never underestimate his power and desire to destroy.

Chapter 7

Enhancing Church Safety And Security Utilizing Surveillance/Security Cameras

Robert M. Cirtin, B.A., M.A.

The use of surveillance/security cameras is a sensitive subject that has elicited much controversy and debate in our society. The use of these cameras in church facilities is even more sensitive.

However, we are talking about the church, God's people in God's house. We pray that the staff and congregation will never come under assault and that a criminal act will never occur. However, we must be prepared to deal with any situation. Video surveillance cameras are appropriate to protect the safety of the public and to detect and deter inappropriate or criminal behavior. This chapter, and in fact this entire book, is devoted to this ideal.

According to David McDonald, CEO of Pelco, in an article published in *ChristianityToday.Com*, surveillance/security cameras may have prevented a gunman from shooting children at a Jewish Community Center in Granada Hills, California, in 1999. McDonald points out that the shooter passed up four other facilities that had closed circuit television systems before choosing a location that did not.

Please know that surveillance cameras may not necessarily be the answer to all church safety and security problems. However, if applied appropriately they can be an excellent tool in achieving a higher level of safety for the staff and congregation. The information obtained through the use of surveillance cameras may not be otherwise available.

Legal Implications

It is not the intent of this chapter to give legal advice. Laws pertaining to civil rights and privacy issues may vary, so each church should consult an attorney who is well versed in the laws of your particular state regarding the use of surveillance cameras.

We know that the Fourth Amendment to the Constitution states:

> *The right of the people to be secure in their persons, houses, papers, and effects, against unreasonable searches and seizures, shall not be violated, and no Warrants shall issue, but upon probable cause, supported by Oath or affirmation, and particularly describing the place to be searched, and the persons or things to be seized.*

How does this apply to the placement of surveillance cameras in the church facility? The issue at hand is a person's right to privacy. The Supreme Court ruled in *Katz vs. United States* that "the Fourth Amendment protects people and not places" and furthermore, "what a person knowingly exposes to the public, even in his own home or office, is not a subject of Fourth Amendment protection." The view of the courts, therefore, is that video surveillance does not violate the Fourth Amendment.

The use of video surveillance is appropriate if it does not violate a person's reasonable expectation of privacy. In effect, this means that a church can place surveillance cameras in places such as hallways, private offices, parking lots, and other public areas. Surveillance cameras cannot be installed in places where there is an expectation of privacy such as restrooms, locker rooms, or other changing areas.

Additionally, some courts have ruled that if the public were unaware of the presence of surveillance cameras, it might be a violation of the Fourth Amendment. Displaying signs to notify the public that surveillance cameras are in use may be a legal component in the use of surveillance cameras in some states.

It is important to ensure that the presence of surveillance cameras do not indicate to the public that they will be rescued if they are the victim of a criminal event. In this vein, decoy cameras should not be used. A decoy camera can provide a deterrent effect in some situations, however, it can also create liability for the church if it leads people to believe that their rescue is imminent if attacked.

Why Should A Church Use Security/Surveillance Cameras?

The use of surveillance cameras can play a vital role in enhancing the safety and security of the staff and congregation and provide a peace of mind to those who enter the church campus. Many people feel safer in church than they would elsewhere, thereby naturally letting down their guard. It is for this reason that church staffs and congregations are easy targets for those who wish to engage in inappropriate or illegal behavior.

Church leadership will want to balance the safety and security of the congregation and church staff as well as the congregation's sensibilities regarding the use of security cameras. As mentioned previously, there is a current debate in our society regarding the use of surveillance cameras and their intrusiveness into people's lives. Church leadership will want to address this issue in terms of the safety of the congregation and staff versus the lack of privacy. Most people will accept the use of security cameras, but it is likely there will also be some in your congregation who are uncomfortable with their presence.

Another issue to be addressed by church leadership is to decide if the purpose of security cameras is prevention or apprehension. In other words, is the presence of security cameras to prevent harmful or illegal acts or do you want the presence of security cameras to assist in apprehending the offenders of such acts? The obvious answer is both, but this issue will direct you as to the type of cameras used in specific locations throughout the church facility.

When addressing the use of surveillance cameras in schools, the National Institute of Justice determined that they can provide a deterrent to inappropriate or criminal behavior. The purpose is to convince people not to attempt to commit behavior that is unacceptable. If in fact someone commits such an act, the evidence obtained through the use of surveillance cameras can be preserved on tape. Even if there is no desire to involve law enforcement, a surveillance camera can assist in identifying and apprehending the perpetrator. Typically, when someone is confronted with videotape evidence — even if the resolutions and detail may not be the quality required to be admissible in court — a confession will result.

In addition, the evidence that a video recording provides can be an invaluable tool in situations involving claims of liability against the church. Even though there may be occasions when this type of evidence can be used against the church, it still serves the purpose of assisting the church in the pursuit of the truth in situations that occur on church property.

The Application Of Surveillance Cameras

The visibility of cameras can be divided into four different applications. Covert cameras will not be seen by the public, overt cameras are positioned in plain view of the public, and some cameras may be concealed in a plastic dome or other means to conceal the camera. In addition, there are also specialty cameras that can be concealed in various devices such as a working wall clock, clock radio, exit sign, fire sprinkler head, smoke detector, flood light, and speakers, just to name a few. There are also cameras available that have very small lenses, including pinhole lenses, and infrared cameras that can be used in some low light environments.

There are many different types of cameras in terms of their application and capabilities. In some areas of your church structure you will need cameras that can view a long hallway, and others will need to capture more of a wide angle picture. An entire new industry has arisen in the past few years that specialize in covert cameras for a variety of applications.

Cameras are available for filming in color as well as in black and white. Cameras that capture a scene in color, however, are more expensive than black and white. Their use will depend on the purpose of the camera.

Microphones are included with some cameras, but according to the National Institute of Justice, caution is advised in their use due to state laws regarding the privacy of conversations.

There are two types of camera configurations currently available: the fixed camera and the pan-tilt-zoom camera. Fixed cameras are mounted on a stationary position and will capture the same scene unless it is relocated. The scene can be recorded and/or viewed on a monitor by church personnel, and since they are much less expensive than pan-tilt-zoom cameras, they are probably the best application for churches. Not only may the expense be cost prohibitive, pan-tilt-zoom cameras require personnel to monitor them. Churches may want to consider a combination of the two based on what is required for specific areas.

Pan-tilt-zoom cameras can operate in two different modes. The most useful mode is for the camera to be controlled by an operator viewing the scene on a monitor. The operator can control the direction and angle of the camera, as well as zoom in on a specific area or person, depending on the situation. A pan-tilt-zoom camera can also be placed in automatic mode which allows the camera to automatically scan over a certain area. If the pan-tilt-zoom cameras are operated in an automatic mode there is a chance that the camera may be pointing in the wrong direction in case of an incident. Also, because the pan-tilt-zoom cameras are mechanical in nature, they require regular maintenance which will add to the operating cost.

The video recorder used to visually capture the activity must also be hidden from view. This can sometimes be rather difficult depending on the location. The video recorder is obviously larger than the camera and also requires ventilation, a relatively clean environment, and must be accessible. There are two ways that the video signal is transmitted to the video recorder. The typical application involves the use of coaxial cable. However, there are also wireless systems that simplify installation. The only concern with wireless applications is that there is a limit to their range of transmission and they are more expensive to purchase.

Another consideration is whether you are going to keep the videotapes for a certain period of time or use a system that constantly recycles the tapes every so often, (such as every 48 or 72 hours). The answer to this question is based on what you want to accomplish by using video cameras.

Again, the type of camera used depends on the desired effect, prevention or apprehension, and the comfort level of the congregation. Additionally, your church may not wish to utilize surveillance cameras on a continual basis but only when an occasional need arises. For example, lets say that the office staff discovered that items are missing from one of the church offices, or personal items were stolen from the choir room while the service was in progress. You may wish to install a temporary covert surveillance camera and videotape recorder to capture anyone who might be responsible for the thefts. If the theft occurred from an office, you can install a video camera concealed in a pencil sharpener, clock, or other covert item on the market that would be present in a typical office. With regard to locations such as the choir room, a covert clock camera, smoke detector, or something similar can be utilized. There are many different kinds of covert cameras available.

In some cases, a typical camcorder can be used by hiding it in an air duct or some other hidden location so it cannot be seen. Surveillance cameras can also be installed with timers to turn on at various times or with motion detectors that will activate when someone enters a room.

After identifying the perpetrator, the church can decide to confront the individual and deal with the matter internally or contact the police and provide the videotape as evidence for prosecution. Church leadership will need to weigh the circumstances and the person involved in order to make this determination.

How To Get Started

Purchasing the appropriate equipment can be an overwhelming experience. There is a plethora of surveillance equipment currently on the market, and like all technology, research and development is continuous. The complexity of the system you need will dictate options on how to secure the appropriate equipment. There are many excellent companies accessible on the Internet that can sell anything you need and provide some level of technical support. You may want to start there in order to become knowledgeable of the type of equipment available.

There are also many companies who sell, install, and support surveillance equipment. It is suggested that you consult with a company who has a track record of providing surveillance systems similar to your church facility. For example, if your church consists of a large structure or possibly a multiple-building complex, you should hire a company who has installed surveillance systems in that type of structure. Some companies may claim that they can provide the services you need but this may not be their strength.

The ultimate usability of videotape recordings is dependent on several variables. There are surveillance systems on the market that provide such a low quality tape recording that the subjects are unidentifiable and their actions indiscernible. It is important for the church to adequately research the various types of surveillance cameras currently available.

Suggested Locations
For Surveillance Cameras

I conducted a survey of some of the largest churches in the United States with regard to their application of surveillance cameras. This resulted in a list of locations where surveillance cameras are most frequently installed. The following is a prioritized list of locations for surveillance cameras based on the most frequent placement.

Hallways

By placing security cameras in the hallways of the church you will be able to capture anyone circulating the building. Depending on the placement of the cameras, this may capture some entrances to the building. You may wish to utilize a combination of overt and covert cameras. Overt cameras will show the public, including those who may consider inappropriate or criminal acts, that the church takes their safety very seriously and has taken steps to provide for their safety.

Entrances

Installing surveillance cameras at the entrances of the building will allow you to see anyone who enters or leaves the building. Although this is an important application of surveillance cameras, this type of camera alone will obviously not capture what occurs throughout the building. Security cameras at the entrances will assist in identifying possible perpetrators. Depending on the desired effect, you can use covert or overt, or a combination of both can be used.

Nursery/preschool areas

Suppose one of the parents of a broken home enters the church to pick up a child but this parent does not have legal custody or any right to do so. Hopefully, your church has taken precautions to ensure that every child is given to the appropriate person as discussed in chapter 4. However, security cameras that target the entrance to the nursery or children's Sunday school area can prove valuable in serving as a deterrent to this type of activity, but they can also assist law enforcement officials in apprehending the perpetrator and returning the child to the parent or legal guardian. These cameras should be overt and in plain view of anyone who approaches areas where children are present. The cameras may serve as a deterrent to inappropriate or illegal activity.

Offices

The church offices present many opportunities for inappropriate behavior such as the theft of church property. Having overt surveillance cameras located in strategic areas can deter inappropriate behavior and assist in the apprehension of those involved. Additionally, in the event an intruder enters the church offices, surveillance cameras will document the incident for investigation and possible criminal prosecution of the intruder. It is also suggested that an overt camera be placed at the entrance of the main office area to serve as a deterrent to inappropriate behavior. If apprehension of a perpetrator is desired, you may wish to use a covert camera housed in a clock, smoke detector, pencil sharpener, or some other covert method.

Parking lots

The church parking lot is obviously a place where criminal acts occur, typically theft from vehicles and theft of vehicles. Since cars are usually unprotected, many criminals recognize a church parking lot as an easy target. Cars have continually been stolen and burglarized while parked in the church parking lot during services.

By placing overt surveillance cameras focused on the church parking lot, a deterrent effect will be realized. In the event of illegal behavior, they will provide evidence to apprehend the perpetrator.

It is suggested that the cameras used in parking lots are the type that provide the ability to rotate and focus on a particular area of the parking lot.

The surveillance cameras targeting parking lots will act in concert with the security officer program discussed in chapter 6.

The perimeter of the building

Surveillance cameras located at the perimeter of the church property will capture anyone before they enter the building through either doors or windows. These are typically targeted outside of the building.

Safe or lockbox used to store money and other valuables

Any place where valuable items are secured, such as offering receipts, should be monitored by a surveillance camera. It is suggested that an overt camera be used in order to serve as an obvious deterrent to any would-be thief. Also, having a surveillance camera in the room where the offering is counted and processed provides a level of security protection to those who handle money.

Platform

Some churches have a surveillance camera targeting the platform. This may consist of a remote-controlled camera that can capture activity on the platform and in the congregation. This allows the operator of the camera to focus in on possible problem areas should an incident occur. This camera can also be used to spot individuals in the congregation who may pose a problem, and to document an incident should it ultimately occur.

Conclusion

The purpose of this chapter is to provoke thought and discussion regarding surveillance systems and to provide practical suggestions as to their use. Again, it is suggested that you consult with a reputable company who has proven experience in providing security camera systems to buildings similar to your facility. For example, if your church consists of a large structure or possibly a multiple-building complex, you should hire a company who has installed security systems in that type of structure. Be aware that there are some companies who will claim that they can provide the equipment and services you need but this may not indeed be their strength. Arming yourself with the information contained in this chapter, you are better equipped to obtain what best suits the needs of your church.

Chapter 8

How To Conduct
A Proper Investigation

Robert M. Cirtin, B.A., M.A.

An investigation in our church? Why would anyone need to know how to conduct an investigation in a church setting? Suppose a member of your congregation came to *you*, a leader (pastor, denominational leader) in your church, and said that he or she was aware of an inappropriate relationship between another staff member and a parishioner. Or maybe the inappropriate relationship is between the senior pastor and a staff member or parishioner. The first question that may come to your mind is if it is necessary to implement an active inquiry to determine if the allegation is true. This is the easy part. The answer is, "Yes!" The next step in the process is the more difficult part: how to go about doing it.

George Washington said, "Truth will ultimately prevail where there are pains taken to bring it to light." Conducting investigations in church situations is a very delicate matter. It is understandable that many church leaders may consider this chapter unnecessary or even "overkill" in dealing with incidents that occur in relation to the church. This sentiment is based on the fact that, quite possibly, up to this point in time nothing has happened in their churches that requires any type of fact-finding endeavor.

However, the biggest fear of church leaders in this regard is possibly upsetting or alienating members of the congregation or staff by making false allegations or possibly being unable to positively prove allegations that appear to have merit. This fear is well founded; as a pastor or church staff member, you certainly do not want to offend anyone. Furthermore, you also want to avoid liability in making allegations that are not supported by facts. Nevertheless, the best way to protect the congregation — as well as members of the paid and volunteer staff — is to determine if the allegations are true or false. This is your spiritual and legal responsibility.

There are many techniques that church leadership can employ to conduct a thorough investigation. Since most church leaders are not professional investigators trained in the art of the investigative process (collecting evidence, interviewing witnesses, and the like), this chapter attempts to provide some simple concepts — illustrating practical and proven techniques — that can be utilized to systematically obtain the information required to determine how best to gather evidence that is relevant to a given situation.

The Investigative Process

The key to a successful investigation is good planning and organization. The fact-finding process will be greatly facilitated by a systematic series of steps known as the *investigative plan*. There may be several different ways to organize the investigative process. The long-standing concept of "who, what, when, where, how, and why" is still a good formula for conducting investigations. Simply enough, when you answer these questions, the investigation is completed. However, accomplishing this requires knowledge, planning, and a process permeated with honesty and integrity. Preparing this style of investigation plan requires four steps, which we will now discuss.

The Investigative Plan

The first step — review all written materials
After becoming aware of an incident or situation in which obtaining additional information is required, the first step in the investigative process is to review any written information that may have already been generated by the person who lodged the complaint. In legal terms this person is known as the *complainant* and may or may not be the person directly involved in the situation

under investigation but may have firsthand knowledge of the situation. This material may consist of memoranda, e-mails, notes, letters, reports, or other documentation.

It is a good practice to require individuals who wish to make a complaint against a staff member or volunteer worker to document their allegations in writing. This will provide formality to the process, provide written documentation, and prevent gossip and innuendoes from being mistaken for facts. It also puts the individual "on the record" which in most cases will prevent some people from making false allegations or spreading rumors. Depending on the nature of the allegations, you may wish to disregard complaints in which the complainant or victim refuses to document their allegation(s) in writing. However, be cautious in making this decision because there may be a legitimate reason why the person feels uncomfortable with putting the information in writing.

As you review the written information, you are gaining an understanding of the allegation(s) and seeing how to respond and proceed through the investigative process. If no such documentation exists, you will need to obtain this initial information from the person alleging the wrongdoing, either the complainant or the victim. It is suggested that you generate notes based on the information provided by the person asserting the allegations. This will give you a basis on which to build the investigation plan.

The second step — identify possible witnesses

Either the written materials received from the complainant or victim (if they exist) or your notes generated from your initial contact with the complainant or victim will assist you in composing a list of possible witnesses who can provide details of the alleged acts. You are particularly interested in those who have firsthand information. (This is the next step in the process.) This may include anyone who was working or in the building at the time of the incident, people who know the suspected perpetrator (relatives, friends), people who were directly affected by the incident or those whom the victim told about the incident. When completed, the people on the list are a good place to begin interviewing.

The third step — formulating relevant questions

After you establish the initial list of possible witnesses, the third step is to begin formulating relevant questions to be asked of each witness. This facilitates organization of the interviews, which greatly enhances the quantity and quality of information you are able to obtain. We will discuss how to construct and ask questions later in this chapter. Again, organization is key, and "winging it" — merely thinking of questions off the top of your head at the time of the interview — will jeopardize the quality of the interviews as well as the results of the investigation. The consequences of the findings of a given investigation could be quite serious and important, and good preparation will lend itself toward clear thinking, and will thus benefit the entire investigation. Certainly, it would be difficult to underestimate the importance of good planning in an investigation.

The initial list of questions just mentioned should serve as a mere beginning, and you should not limit yourself to only asking the questions that appear on your list. They are based only on the information you have initially, and information will be developed as the interview proceeds. You will also want to ask clarifying questions, follow-up questions, and questions that you thought of during the interview based on what the person discloses. For example, suppose you are interviewing a witness regarding an allegation of employee theft. As the interview progresses, the interviewee provides information, which indicates that possibly more than one employee is involved. The interviewer should pursue this further by asking questions that will encourage the person to discuss what they know about anyone else involved. This can be accomplished of course by asking follow-up and clarifying questions, as well as questions you will develop in relation to the information the interviewee has already provided.

It is necessary to be aware that as the investigation progresses, the list of witnesses may grow as you obtain additional information. It should be expected that, as you continually interview more and more witnesses, they will most likely provide the names of others of whom you are unaware who may have knowledge of the incident and should, therefore, be interviewed as well.

Furthermore, it should also be realized that the person you are interviewing may take you down a path that was hitherto unknown to you. For example, the interviewee may provide information about the person you are investigating that you did not formerly know; they may also provide information about other individuals involved in the incident you are investigating. Investigations sometimes progress in directions that are quite unexpected, and sometimes unseemly. You should, however, *always* pursue *all* relevant leads.

Many of the situations that may require an investigation may be very sensitive and embarrassing for those involved. This cannot prevent the investigator from obtaining relevant evidence. For example, if you are conducting an investigation into allegations of an inappropriate sexual relationship, it is vital to get very detailed and specific information. In order to prove or disprove the allegations, the investigator must ask about specific sexual acts, when and where they occurred, and how long the relationship lasted, among other questions.

The fourth step — identify possible evidence

The fourth step in the investigation plan, based on the information provided by the complainant, is composing a list of possible evidence that may be secured to assist in proving or disproving the allegations. Depending on the allegation(s) this may include videotape recordings, financial records, photographs, biological fluids, damage to church property committed to further the act, court records, fingerprints, or documentation of previous problems with the alleged perpetrator such as criminal records.

Conducting The Investigation

Interviewing

The time for action has come. All written information has been reviewed that may have been generated by the person who made the complaint, a list of possible witnesses who can provide details of the alleged acts has been composed, relevant questions to be asked of each witness have been formulated, and a list of possible evidence that may be collected to assist in proving or disproving the allegations has been assembled.

Now it is time to begin conducting interviews and collecting relevant evidence. Giving thought to this part of the investigation, you may ask, "Who should I interview first?" It is suggested that the first person to be interviewed is the person who brought the allegations forward. This will be either the complainant or the victim. This is presuming, of course, that the interviewer has not already spoken with the complainant and has relied upon any documentation that may exist. Nevertheless, depending on who made the allegations, the complainant or victim is interviewed first in order to determine what occurred and to develop a set of facts that will determine the course of the investigation.

The purpose of interviewing the complainant (or victim) is to obtain as much information as possible with regard to what happened, who they believe is involved, what information the person is relying on to make the allegation, and what evidence exists to support the allegation. This initial interview will indicate if an investigation is warranted, and if so, will assist in dictating the necessary steps in the investigative process. If it is believed that the allegation(s) has validity, the information provided by the complainant will assist you in determining whether to continue the investigation. For example, the allegations may be asserted by someone who merely misunderstood what they heard or observed. By interviewing this person first, it is possible to avoid the possible harm and embarrassment to all concerned if the information does not warrant an investigation. On the other hand, if the complainant (or victim) provides a very detailed account of what occurred and also provides relevant evidence to support the allegations, this provides the investigator a viable basis in which to continue the investigation and guidance as to the direction the investigation should proceed.

In addition, it is important to clarify the complaint and get additional information that may not have been included in the written complaint materials or was not available when the allegation(s) was submitted. The written documentation that initiated the complaint will never provide sufficient information to prove or disprove the allegations. More is needed. Also, it is important to have the complainant verbally say "on the record" what they are alleging.

The next category of people to interview is witnesses that are involved in or have firsthand knowledge of the situation and can provide information relevant to the allegations. This may include other staff or volunteer workers, people who may have been present or nearby when the incident occurred, or family members of the victim and alleged perpetrator.

You should attempt to prioritize the possible witnesses in the order of their importance. Typically, witnesses fall into one of two categories: primary and secondary. Primary witnesses are those individuals who can provide information about the entire scenario surrounding the incident under investigation. These people can tell the whole story of what happened. Secondary witnesses are those who can provide pieces to the puzzle that make a contribution to determining what occurred. For example, suppose you are investigating allegations that a volunteer Sunday school worker physically struck a child. Primary witnesses may include anyone who observed the incident occur such as another Sunday school worker, a parent, other children who were present, and even the child who was assaulted (depending on their ages). Secondary witnesses may include someone who heard the child cry after the incident, or anyone to whom the child may have reported the incident.

At this point the investigation is proceeding per your own investigative plan. You continue to follow all relevant leads, interview witnesses, and collect evidence until you exhaust all possibilities in these categories.

Finally, it is important that the person who is accused of committing the inappropriate or illegal behavior is interviewed last. In police vernacular, this person is called the suspect. In more socially acceptable language, we call this person the *respondent*.

The interview of the respondent is greatly facilitated if you are equipped with as much information as possible about what is alleged to have occurred. Having interviewed the complainant, victim, and witnesses provides detailed knowledge of the allegations and will allow the interviewer to ask intelligent questions based on the facts already established; it will allow the interviewer to counter information provided by the respondent; it will also provide a full, complete picture of what happened, which is beneficial when formulating questions to be asked of the respondent.

In preparing to interview the respondent, it is important to bear in mind that there are two sides to every story. After all, the allegations may not be true, and it is both ethical and democratic to hear the respondent's explanation. Moreover, suspects in a court of law are innocent until proven guilty. On the other hand, however, the allegations you are investigating may indeed be true, and being prepared for what the respondent may say will facilitate the quality of the investigation in getting to the truth.

There is a possibility that the interview with the respondent may conclude the investigation. However, there may be some follow-up or "cleanup" interviews to conduct. This may include people whom the respondent requests that you interview who may provide relevant information on his behalf, and those you identify who may verify or refute information provided by the respondent.

Interview techniques

It is realized that the readers of this book are not trained and experienced investigators or interviewers. Therefore, it is the intent of this section to provide a few practical guidelines that will assist church leaders in asking the right questions in the right way. There are certain basic interview techniques that will facilitate obtaining accurate information.

As previously mentioned, conducting good interviews is more than just asking, "What happened?" It is very important to take a rather large portion of time to prepare for the interviews in order to get the information you need.

Some knowledge of basic interview techniques can make all the difference in the world in getting to the truth of the matter under investigation. For a variety of reasons, most people may not automatically tell you what you need to know. For example:

- They may not want to tell you because they do not want to

get involved
- They may be hesitant to incriminate themselves or someone else
- They may not remember details unless you prompt them with questions
- Possibly the person does not know what information you need

Here are a few practical suggestions that will improve the quality of your interviews and, therefore, facilitate getting to the truth of the matter at hand.

- Interview one person at a time. Attempting to interview more than one person during the same session will cause confusion in ascertaining the facts, inhibit truthful information because some witnesses may not want others to know what they are saying, and by allowing the witnesses to "compare notes," some people may provide information for which they do not have firsthand knowledge.
- Set a positive tone. Convey confidence that you are competent in conducting the investigation and that all you are trying do is to get to the truth of the matter under investigation.
- It is appropriate to ask, "What happened?" but this is not enough. You should ask specific, detailed questions for each person you interview based on complaint documentation and information provided by other witnesses.
- The interview should be conducted in a conversational dialogue approach. You will want to have a non-confrontational dialogue with the person being interviewed.
- Ask open-ended questions and avoid close-ended questions. In other words, you should ask questions that require the person to provide information and not be able to answer a question by responding "Yes" or "No." "Yes or No" answers will not obtain the information you need.
- The location of the interviews is imperative. It is suggested

that the investigator control the location of the interview. It is best to conduct the interview in a location comfortable for all parties involved, such as an office or someone's home. Avoid conducting interviews in public places, such as restaurants, where privacy is not afforded. The location should instill confidence in the interviewee that the matter is taken seriously and that their well-being and privacy is considered important. However, a word of caution. As the person conducting the investigation, you need to control the investigative process and the final decision as to the location of the interview is up to you. Avoid allowing the interviewee to control this aspect of the investigation to his advantage.

In order to get the most out of your interview, the manner in which you ask questions can determine the quality of the information obtained. The key to this aspect is question phraseology: there is always more than one way to ask a question. Here are some simple guidelines:

- Do not ask questions in a manner that suggests an answer. In an attempt to be helpful, inexperienced interviewers may unwittingly try to assist the interviewee with their responses. The problem is that the person may accept and use your answer instead of giving his own answer. Obviously, this inhibits the impartial, unbiased pursuit of truth.

   To illustrate, the following is an example of an incorrect way to ask this questions is: *"Why did you take the money from the church secretary's desk? Was it because you needed the money?"*

   A better way to ask the same question that does not suggest an answer is as follows: *"Could you tell me why you took the money from the church secretary's desk?"*

   The second question does not suggest a certain answer (it is not a "leading" question) and requires the interviewee to provide his/her own answer. In addition, the question is open-ended and cannot be answered with a

"Yes or No" response.

- Another consideration is that there may be a need to obtain confirmation of information you have already developed, such as facts that have already been proven by corroborating witnesses or evidence. This is especially applicable when interviewing the respondent. When this is the case, you may want to use more *assumptive question phraseology*. Assumptive question phraseology assumes certain facts in order to obtain a truthful response from the interviewee. Don't forget, this is based on facts that have already been *proven* in your investigation by corroborating witnesses, evidence, or a combination of the two. Here's an example:

  The incorrect way to ask this question is: *"Pastor, did you have sexual relations with Judy Jones?"*

  When asked in this manner you can expect a stern denial. The exception, of course, is when the subject of the investigation has decided to cooperate and admit to their wrongdoing. Although we hope this will occur, it is typically not the case.

  A better way to ask this question is the following: *"Pastor, would you please tell me the details of when you and Judy Jones had sexual relations last month?"*

  The second question, based on facts already proven, implicitly assumes that the sexual behavior did in fact occur, and, therefore, the only question is what specifically occurred, when did it occur, how often, and other details. As has been seen, specificity in questioning is of the utmost importance.

- When asking questions, you need to obtain specific, detailed information even when the subject matter is sensitive, deviant, or embarrassing. It is not adequate, for example, for a witness or respondent to merely admit that they had extramarital sexual relations. Much more specificity is needed. In today's world, the term "sexual relations" has different meanings to different people. Therefore, the interviewer must extract specific details describing the acts that were committed regardless of the sensitivity of the allegations.

- When interviewing the respondent and the allegations are already proven, it is best to prevent the person from flatly denying the allegations. This is because the more times a person denies the allegations, the more difficult it is to get them to change their account to state what is actually the truth.
- Finally, before you end an interview with all witnesses, always ask if they know of anyone else who could provide information about the situation. This is a way to develop further leads to be pursued. Most of the time they will tell you.

Collecting evidence

As a church leader, you are not required to obtain evidence in the legal and constitutional manner that is required of law enforcement officials. However, there are some simple guidelines that should be followed that can enhance the quality of the investigation, afford the individuals involved a fair process, and assist in your pursuit of the truth. It may help you to understand some basic concepts pertaining to evidence and evidence collection.

There are essentially three types of evidence: information from witnesses, documentary evidence, and physical evidence. Because the goal of an investigation is to prove or disprove the allegations, the use of real, meaningful evidence is crucial. We will now examine these three types of evidence.

Witness information

We have already addressed information received from witnesses; this is one form of evidence. The information obtained through interviews should be documented in a written report generated by the person who conducted the interview. The investigative report should be maintained in a secured manner such as a locking filing cabinet or a safe. If the person under investigation is an employee or volunteer, a copy of the investigative report should be maintained in their personnel file. It is imperative to maintain strict confidentiality and security of these types of documents. It is recommended that all interviews be audiotape recorded. Depending on the state in which you are conducting the investigation, you may be able to covertly tape-record interviews. Some states allow covert tape-recording as long as one person involved in the conversation is aware that the interview is being recorded. (This would be the interviewer.) However, in several states it is illegal to secretly record a conversation unless all parties are aware that it is being tape-recorded. It is, therefore, highly advisable to consult an attorney in your state who can provide direction in this regard.

Of course, the interviewer can ask permission of the person being interviewed to tape-record the interview. However, with a tape recorder present, many times the person may be reluctant to provide complete, candid, or truthful information for fear that someone else may hear the tape in the future.

Documentary evidence

Documentary evidence consists of any document that provides information that is relevant to the allegations. According to *Black's Law Dictionary*, documentary evidence is:

Evidence derived from conventional symbols (such as letters) by which ideas are represented on material substances. Such evidence as is furnished by written instruments, inscriptions, documents of all kinds, and also any inanimate objects admissible for the purpose, as distinguished from "oral" evidence, or that delivered by human beings viva voce.

Essentially, documentary evidence is information that is somehow in written form. This may include printed e-mails, financial records, letters, notes, or greeting cards discussing an inappropriate relationship or financial misconduct. For example, suppose you are investigating allegations that a member of the congregation who is responsible for counting the Sunday offering collection stole money from the Sunday receipts and the person suspected attempted to cash or deposit a check written by a member of the congregation. That check could serve as documentary evidence.

Another cogent example: It is alleged that the senior pastor has been involved in an inappropriate relationship with a member of the church staff and that their meeting place of choice is a hotel in a nearby town. The hotel invoice paid by the pastor could serve as documentary evidence.

Physical evidence

Physical evidence consists of material objects or items that prove a fact. This may include biological specimens (semen, blood, or other fluids), computer disc or hard drive, video and audiotape recordings, fingerprints, weapons, or items left by a perpetrator, just to name a few. Because of the nature of the types of situations related to church matters, physical evidence may not be present. For example, suppose it is alleged that a church staff member is accused of viewing pornographic websites on his church computer. The computer itself could serve as physical evidence.

Collecting and processing evidence

There are correct ways that evidence should be collected, labeled, and packaged. There is not enough space in this chapter to discuss the intricacies of processing evidence in the manner of law enforcement agencies, but many times this is not necessary.

To assist church leaders in conducting investigations, the following guidelines will prove helpful.

Witness information should be written in a report using a narrative format that fully explains in detail what the interviewee stated. The report is not a word-for-word transcript of the interview, but a summary of what was said that fully explains the relevant information possessed by the interviewee. The report should also include certain quotes of relevant information stated by the interviewee. For example, if the allegations pertain to sexual contact by the parties involved, specific, detailed information must be obtained from the person interviewed. Obviously, quoting the interviewee is a good way of documenting this.

All reports must be secured in a locked file cabinet, safe, or other secure area. This will help ensure confidentiality and the security of the information contained in the reports.

Documentary evidence must be secured in a container of some type such as an envelope or plastic covering. Depending on the purpose of the document, it is better to handle it as little as possible. If at all possible, it is better not to fold the document.

The container used to hold the document should have the following labels:

- The name of the person who provided the document as evidence
- The name of the person who obtained the document
- The date the document was collected
- A description of the document written on the outside of the container
- The location from which the document was seized

Physical evidence sometimes requires special handling. If physical evidence is present, and the incident is also a crime (addressed later), it is suggested your local law enforcement agency be contacted to process the evidence. It may be advisable to consult with law enforcement personnel to assist in the collection of any physical evidence. If you choose to collect evidence yourself, here are a few guidelines that may be helpful:

- If the evidence is wet due to some type of liquid on it, always place it in paper packaging such as an envelope or grocery bag, depending on the size of the object. Never place wet items in a plastic container because they may mold or mildew and destroy the integrity of the evidence. If the item of evidence was wet but had dried, you may place it in a plastic container such as a zip-lock type bag.
- If you are collecting liquid evidence such as semen, use a piece of clean, dry, white 100 percent cotton cloth to soak up the liquid and then place it in a paper container such as an envelope or small paper bag.
- After placing the item of evidence in the appropriate con-

tainer, seal the container with some type of tape and write your name and the date on the tape. By doing this, if someone tampers with the evidence, it will be noticeable. Then, write the following information somewhere on the container:

- The name of the person who provided the item of evidence
- The name of the person who collected the evidence
- The date the evidence was collected
- A description of the evidence written on the outside of the container
- The location from which the evidence was seized
- As with any type of evidence, it is very important to secure it in a locked file cabinet, safe, or other locked container.

Sources of evidence

Evidence can come from a variety of different sources, which vary according to the nature of the investigation. The following consists of a general list of sources from which evidence may be found:

- The complainant may have physical, documentary, or other evidence to submit with their information.
- Witnesses may also provide evidence that proves the allegations.
- The person under investigation may be able to provide evidence, but may also be reluctant to provide evidence unless it disproves the allegations.
- Financial records of the church or that of the person under investigation.
- Computers can reveal information that is relevant to the allegations.
- Governmental agencies will provide information that is available to the general public such as criminal convictions, civil litigation, or licensure information including disciplinary actions.
- Attorneys who possess information that may be relevant

to the investigation as long as releasing the information benefits their client.

- Medical and/or mental health records of someone involved in the allegations. (Note: These records can only be obtained through consent of the patient or a court order.)
- Security camera tape recordings (if available).

Other methods to obtain relevant evidence

- **Use of polygraph examinations** — Although polygraph examinations may not be appropriate for all situations, it is still an excellent investigative tool. If the investigation lacks other types of evidence to support the allegation, and you still believe there is merit to the allegation, a request to polygraph the parties involved may obtain truthful information. Many times a mere request of the victim, witness, or person under investigation to submit to a polygraph examination may cause that person to provide truthful information without even having the actual polygraph test administered.

- **Forensic computer data recovery** — Another very useful tool that can be successful in gaining a plethora of information is forensic computer data recovery. The reason is deceptively simple: nothing is ever truly deleted from a computer. Some computer experts possess the technology and the ability to extract information from a computer's hard drive even though the user deleted it. Much inappropriate and deviant behavior involves the use of e-mail and certain websites, most involving pornography. Evidence the perpetrator would think to have been deleted can, in actuality, be detected and retrieved by forensic computer data recovery. This technology can be a tremendous source of evidence in some investigations. For example, my company, Robert Cirtin Investigations, once conducted an investigation in which the subject's wife suspected that her husband was having an inappropriate relationship with another woman. The initial evidence consisted of one e-mail received by her husband but she could find no other evidence because her husband deleted all other e-mails. We conducted forensic computer data recovery on the computer, which discovered numerous e-mails to, and from, the individuals involved as well as several pornographic websites her husband had visited which evidenced the inappropriate relationship. Additionally, there has been a proliferation of Internet pornography used by many members of society, which unfortunately has included many church leaders. Forensic computer data recovery can be helpful in uncovering this in order to begin the restorative and rehabilitative process for the person involved.

Documenting the details of the investigation is one of the more significant aspects of the investigative process. The typical manner in which to document the investigation is to generate some type of written report. The report should document every step in the investigative process which may include the following:

- The names and personal information such as address and telephone number of all victims, witnesses, and respondent
- A detailed account of what each person said in his respective interviews
- A description of all relevant evidence used to prove or disprove the allegations
- The results of the investigation

It is crucial to maintain confidentiality of all information obtained in the investigation. Therefore, written reports should be secured in a locking file cabinet or some other locked container. It is also a good idea to have more than one copy of the report kept in a location different from the original report. Furthermore, it is important to secure computer files and discs to ensure confidentiality.

Maintaining objectivity

It is imperative that those conducting an investigation maintain objectivity and impartiality during the investigative process. At the outset, you are dealing with allegations. It is your job to prove or disprove them by using, as Joe Friday frequently said, "Just the facts." The investigator must resist the temptation to rush to judgment because doing so will taint the investigative process. As stated previously, the purpose of the investigation is to prove or disprove the allegations. Therefore, the investigator must not approach the fact-finding process with a closed mind, predisposed to a specific version of the facts, or assuming facts that have not been proven. Even though the development of facts and evidence may point to a certain conclusion as the investigation proceeds, the investigator must maintain objectivity in order to ensure the quality of the investigation.

Completing the investigation

Sometimes it is difficult to determine when to end the investigation and decide how much information is enough information. To resolve this question, it is necessary to determine if there is enough evidence to prove or disprove the allegations. If there is, the investigation is completed. If there is not, continue the investigation as long as there are leads to pursue. It is important to all concerned that the investigator has been thorough, scientific, and careful in the investigation and that he has earnestly, objectively, and impartially pursued the truth. As we noted previously, the key to a successful investigation is good planning, preparation, and organization. If this occurs, it is likely that you will discover the truth.

Final Considerations

An investigation is a pursuit of, and inquiry into, the truth. Sometimes church leaders are more concerned about their own reputation, and that of the church, than with sincerely pursuing the truth and then appropriately responding to any uncovered wrongdoing. We know from previous high-profile incidents involving religious leaders, as well as some political leaders, that ensures us that a cover-up of the situation will always prove more detrimental to all involved than shedding light on the truth. This requires a demonstration of genuine integrity that is required to do the right thing.

Yet another significant consideration remains. Churches have been successfully sued by individuals when it was proven that wrongdoing was known by church leadership but nothing was done to deal with the matter. Conducting a thorough investigation will provide a good defense in a civil lawsuit for failure to act when inappropriate or illegal behavior is alleged.

Additionally, if the situation for which an investigation is necessary constitutes a crime, call your local law enforcement agency. The church may also elect to conduct their own independent investigation, but if the incident is also a violation of criminal law, you must involve the police.

Finally, please know that there may be some situations for which an investigation should not be attempted by church or denominational leaders. For example, if there is an allegation of child abuse or child sexual abuse, this should be reported to government officials who are entrusted with the responsibility of investigating these types of issues. They are trained and experienced in investigative techniques, such as interviewing and evidence collection, that has a positive effect on both the victim and the accused. The church may then utilize their findings to take any actions deemed appropriate.

Incidents involving children are unique, and trained professionals are required to successfully extract truthful information and determine what occurred. The number of times a victim of child abuse and child sexual abuse is interviewed should be limited in order to avoid compounding the trauma they experience. Therefore, interviews should be conducted only by professionals who are trained in interviewing children in these types of situations.

There may be some resistance on the part of church leadership to involve civil authorities such as law enforcement or government agencies charged with dealing with these types of situations. The concern of church leadership may arise from wanting to avoid negative publicity for the church and the denomination. However, the fair and proper treatment of the victim and alleged offender is the primary concern, which will in turn enhance the quality of the investigation and, of course, assist in the pursuit of the truth, which is always good for the church, for society, and for the individual. Those formally involved in conducting an investigation in their own churches would do well to remember the words of former Wyoming senator Alan Simpson, who once said, "If you have integrity, nothing else matters; if you don't have integrity, nothing else matters."

Endorsements

I trust Bob Cirtin. He knows what to do to help keep people safe. I'm glad he's on our side, enabling us to better protect the people God has entrusted to our care. Our congregants have the right to feel secure when they come to God's house. This book will help us achieve this for our people.

John E. Marshall
Senior Pastor, Second Baptist Church
Springfield, Missouri

What a sacred privilege it is to care for God's people! But while we focus on their spiritual needs, we must not forget their safety needs — especially in our world today. I'm excited to see a book that identifies the real security issues every church faces. We need to implement these proactive steps to ensure a higher level of safety for our flock. And we need to send a reassuring message to those in our communities who want to come.

Chuck Lynch
Pastor of Spiritual Development, Victory Church
Lakeland, Florida

*The church is blessed to have volunteers who want to make a difference in the world with their time and talent. It is imperative that we provide adequate counsel and practical guidance that can maximize their assistance. **Church Safety And Security: A Practical Guide** is an excellent volume, with relevant suggestions for helping a local congregation obey our Lord's mandate to "occupy until I come."*

Robert H. Spence
President, Evangel University

In our present litigious society, churches are in danger from multiple sources. An accident, a crime committed by an unscreened volunteer or employee, an injury resulting from negligence, or a mistake by a leader may expose the congregation to tremendous jeopardy. However, there is a simple and reasonable defense:

*preparation! Congregates and courts alike do not require that our churches be totally safe with accident-free programs and perfect employees. But they do expect church leaders to take reasonable precautions to protect attendees. At this point, **Church Safety and Security: A Practical Guide** becomes a valuable resource. Bob Cirtin has the unusual but important background mixture of service in full-time church ministry, a certified officer of the law, and an expert investigator. He has personal experience with every source of danger for the local church and has developed effective safeguards and defenses. His strategies are clear, simple, easy to implement, and will protect any congregation in the event of an unfortunate event. This book is a must for every church office and library. I am pleased and eager to recommend it to every pastor!*

Terry Raburn
Superintendent, Peninsular Florida District Council
Assemblies of God

If you are a pastor, associate pastor, preschool director, church school principal, deacon, elder, vestryperson, or denominational leader — read this book! Then, read it again! Make it required reading for every leader in your church. Protect your congregation, your property, and your reputation in the community by doing all you can do to hire the right employees, to prevent physical and sexual misconduct for which your church may be liable, and to reduce the legal and financial impacts of such misconduct. This book will teach you what to look for, and how to take action today to protect the people God has given you to shepherd.

Tom Duncan
Associate Pastor, Anglican Church of the Resurrection
St. Louis, Missouri

This is a book written for our changing times, when the security of our churches must become a priority. Written by professionals who have a strong Christian influence in their lives, this book is a great tool for the security program of your church.

Jack L. Merritt
Sheriff, Greene County, Missouri
Retired Capt., Missouri State Highway Patrol

About The Authors

Robert M. Cirtin is an assistant professor and director of the criminal justice program at Evangel University in Springfield, Missouri. He is also the founder and president of Robert Cirtin Investigations, a company providing professional investigative and consulting services to churches, businesses, and government agencies. A former police officer and Missouri state investigator who has also served in full-time ministry, Cirtin is a frequent guest lecturer on a variety of safety and security topics. He is a graduate of Central Bible College and Lincoln University.

John M. Edie is the executive pastor of Second Baptist Church in Springfield, Missouri, where he is responsible for facility management, staff coordination, and directing the church's education division. He has served in similar positions at churches in Wichita Falls, Texas, and Shreveport, Louisiana. Edie is a graduate of Southwest Baptist University and Midwestern Baptist Theological Seminary.

Dennis K. Lewis is the director of public safety for the Springfield Public Schools in Springfield, Missouri. He is also the co-founder of EDU-SAFE, an advisory and training organization which assists school administrators and others in providing safe schools. He has co-authored seven books on school safety, and his articles have appeared in several regional and national periodicals. Lewis has also presented numerous workshops and seminars at state and national conferences on school violence and crisis management, and he is a guest lecturer at several universities. He is a graduate of College of the Ozarks and Central Missouri State University.

Edward L. Spain serves as administrative director of neurosciences at St. John's Regional Health Center in Springfield, Missouri. He has authored numerous articles for local and national publications, conducted research into providing care for burn patients, and served as a guest speaker for several state and national seminars. He is a graduate of Southwest Missouri State University and Southwest Baptist University.

Donna M. Washburn is an assistant professor of social work at Evangel University. She is also a licensed clinical social worker who has been a therapist for abused and neglected children in residential, hospital, and outpatient settings. Washburn serves as a consultant on counseling skills and abuse issues for a national faith-based substance abuse organization. She is a graduate of Evangel University and Southwest Missouri State University.